Carlos Andres Loaiza Garcia

Analysis of applications and success factors of cloud computing for small- and medium-sized businesses

GRIN Verlag

Bibliografische Information der Deutschen Nationalbibliothek:

Die Deutsche Bibliothek verzeichnet diese Publikation in der Deutschen National-bibliografie; detaillierte bibliografische Daten sind im Internet über http://dnb.d-nb.de/ abrufbar.

Imprint:

Copyright © 2012 GRIN Verlag GmbH
Druck und Bindung: Books on Demand GmbH, Norderstedt Germany
ISBN: 978-3-656-37159-5

This book at GRIN:

http://www.grin.com/en/e-book/209530/analysis-of-applications-and-success-factors-of-cloud-computing-for-small

GRIN - Your knowledge has value

Der GRIN Verlag publiziert seit 1998 wissenschaftliche Arbeiten von Studenten, Hochschullehrern und anderen Akademikern als eBook und gedrucktes Buch. Die Verlagswebsite www.grin.com ist die ideale Plattform zur Veröffentlichung von Hausarbeiten, Abschlussarbeiten, wissenschaftlichen Aufsätzen, Dissertationen und Fachbüchern.

Visit us on the internet:

http://www.grin.com/

http://www.facebook.com/grincom

http://www.twitter.com/grin_com

Analysis of applications and success factors of cloud computing for small- and medium-sized businesses

(Untersuchung von Cloud Anwendungen und Erfolgsfaktoren von Cloud Computing für kleine und mittelständische Unternehmen)

Carlos Andrés Loaiza García

"We exist for our fellow-men - in the first place for those on whose smiles and welfare all our happiness depends, and next for all those unknown to us personally with whose destinies we are bound up by the tie of sympathy".   Albert Einstein

Lograr este nuevo escalón de mi vida no hubiera sido posible sin el apoyo incondicional de mi esposa, amiga, compañera de viajes, aventuras, y ahora de golf, Jenny.

A mis padres y a mi hermanita, base y columna de todo lo que soy hoy.

A nuestra familia, fuente de apoyo permanente.

A aquellos que nos acompañan en esta aventura llamada vida, a esas personas muy queridas que nos han abandonado en el camino pedroso y polvoriento pero a la vez deslumbrante y maravilloso.

"Los seres humanos no nacen para siempre el día en que sus madres los alumbran: la vida los obliga a parirse a sí mismos una y otra vez, a modelarse, a transformarse, a interrogarse (a veces sin respuesta), a preguntarse para qué diablos han llegado a la tierra y qué deben hacer en ella".
Gabriel García Márquez

KURZFASSUNG

Cloud Computing hat eine große Bedeutung in der Industrie gewonnen, hauptsächlich bei kleinen und mittelständischen Unternehmen, auf Grund der vielen Vorteile im Hinblick auf Kosteneinsparungen, schnellere Produkteinführungszeit, Skalierbarkeit, Flexibilität und Optimierung von Ressourcen.

Heute wird Cloud Computing als die nächste IT-Revolution betrachtet und eine sehr große Anzahl von Artikeln, Bücher, Veröffentlichungen und technischen Berichten steht in der Literaturwelt zur Verfügung.

Im Rahmen dieser Masterarbeit werden die relevantesten Cloud Computing Anwendungen für kleine und mittelständische Unternehmen identifiziert. Zusätlich werden die zentralen Erfolgsfaktoren für die Einführung von Cloud Computing Anwendungen auf Basis der empirischen Untersuchung analysiert, die als Teil der Arbeit durchgeführt wurde.

Schließlich werden sowohl die Vor- und Nachteile der verschiedenen Cloud Computing Modelle, als auch die wichtigsten Ergebnisse der aktuellen Forschung im Cloud Computing Bereich vorgestellt.

ABSTRACT

Cloud computing is gaining importance in the industry and specially within small- and medium-sized companies due to the many benefits in terms of cost savings, faster time to market, scalability, cost flexibility and optimization of resources.

Today, cloud computing is considered as the next IT revolution and the number of articles, books, papers and technical reports flood the literature.

Within the scope of this master thesis, relevant cloud computing applications for small- and medium- sized companies are identified and the key success factors for adoption of cloud computing services are analyzed based on the empirical investigation performed as part of this work.

Finally, the benefits and constraints of the different cloud computing service models are presented including also the state-of-the-art research in the cloud computing area and a summary of the most important results.

CONTENTS

CHAPTER 1

Introduction

1.1 Context

The way people and companies are communicating and interacting with each other is nowadays very different than decades ago. The standalone mainframe solution in charge of processing information was enhanced with client-server solutions. With the propagation of the internet, quick distribution of information and the interworking among systems started playing an important role. Today, new technologies are enabling companies to virtualize the infrastructure and execute applications using the internet, opening immense possibilities of using software and information technologies "in the cloud".

Cloud computing is considered as the next IT revolution as well as just a hype. The term is not only found in several articles, specialized magazines, books and conferences, but it is also a subject widely discussed in the consulting industry.

Focusing on the industry, cloud computing is gaining importance in many small- and medium-sized companies due to the many benefits in terms of cost savings, faster time to market, mobility and flexibility, among others. Additionally, small- and medium-sized companies using cloud computing services can concentrate on the core business and do not need to invest any effort in setting up and running an own infrastructure and software, which can be replaced with cloud computing solutions.

1.2 Objective and structure

In the scope of this master thesis, cloud computing applications for small- and medium-sized companies are identified as well as the key success factors for adoption of cloud computing services are analyzed based on the empirical investigation performed in scope of this work. The advantages and disadvantages of the different cloud computing service models are also presented including the state-of-the-art research in the area. Additionally, an analysis of the acceptance and current usage of cloud computing in small- and medium-sized businesses is included.

This master thesis is divided into seven chapters:

Chapter 1 gives a short introduction and describes the structure of the document.

Chapter 2 gives basic information about the different software applications used in the industry. Additionally, the term cloud computing is introduced as well as the fundamentals of the success factor's theory. Finally, the forms and characteristics of small- and medium-sized businesses are explained.

Chapter 3 presents the state-of-the-art research in cloud computing and summarizes some studies available in the literature, which focus on the cloud computing model and its implementation in different industry branches. The main results concerning applications and key success factors for adoption of cloud computing services are also presented.

Chapter 4 gives information about the empirical investigation performed within the scope of this master thesis and presents the method used and the survey's sample.

Chapter 5 presents the results of the empirical investigate and analyzes the usage of cloud computing solutions and of the most significant cloud applications for small- and medium-sized businesses.

Chapter 6 outlines the key success factors for adoption of cloud computing services based on the empirical investigation.

Chapter 7 summarizes the analysis of applications and success factors for small- and medium-sized business which were analyzed in this master thesis.

1.3   Methods

Diverse specialized literature and internet websites were used for the preparation of this master thesis. The literature used focuses mainly on cloud computing. The most relevant aspects handled in this literature are:

- The implementation and acceptance of cloud computing in different branches
- The relevance of cloud computing as a new option for companies
- The opportunities and risks of using cloud computing from a corporate point of view
- The strategical approach of cloud computing

The complete literature is available in the library of the Bonn-Rhine-Sieg University of Applied Sciences in Rheinbach and Sankt Augustin, Germany.

Many computer related definitions were taken from business informatics books as well as from experienced and specialized magazines prepared by companies with a broad cloud computing theoretical and practical experience like T-Systems. Cloud computing related definitions were taken also from specialized research companies pioneers in the cloud computing area like Gartner research and Forrester research. The websites from salesforce and the "initiative cloud services made in Germany" were also important sources used in this work.

Some investigations already done in the cloud computing area were used within the scope of this master thesis: the diploma thesis investigating the application of cloud computing in E-business[1] gives a good overview to cloud computing and its application; an empirical investigation performed by the Fraunhofer institute[2] related to the application of cloud computing in the health insurance area provides good information about the practical use of cloud computing. This last study gave good guidelines for the empirical studies done in this work.

Finally, an empirical investigation was done as part of the master thesis, which has been performed in cooperation with the cloud services business unit of Deutsche Telekom. The study consisted of an online survey directed to IT decision makers of small- and medium-sized companies. A total of 613 companies had participated in the survey. The main focus of this survey was the identification of relevant cloud computing applications and the key success factors for the adoption of cloud computing services.

---

[1][11]Möller, Christian: Cloud Computing-Einsatz im E-Business, 2010
[2][23]Weidmann, Monika; Renner, Thomas; Rex, Sascha: Cloud computing in der Versicherungsbranche, 2010

CHAPTER 2

Fundamentals

2.1 Fundamentals of software applications

2.1.1 Definition and characteristics

Software applications[1] are used to perform specific tasks using computer systems. In the last years, software applications gained an important role for facilitating the process of many tasks in parallel and improving the efficiency in the companies.

An application software[2] may consist of a single program, such as a specific invoice program or a chat program. It may be also a collection of programs or software packages that interact closely together to accomplish different tasks, such as spreadsheet or text processing functions. This software is commonly known as software suite. There are also very specific software applications used for engineering, process automation or billing processing. Finally, complex software applications used to coordinate the different aspects of the value chain management play a key role in the companies as the different processes are controlled and managed from a unique application.

2.1.2 Type of software applications

Following sections present the most relevant software applications used in a wide range of industries.

2.1.2.1 Email communication

Email communication software[3] allows to send and receive text messages including also files, audio and video independently of the platform used. It is possible to send email messages to different receiver. It is not required that the users are online in order to receive the messages as they are stored in the exchange servers.

Email software is one of the most used applications in companies.

---

[1]See [44] Webopedia, IT Business Edge: Application software definition,
<http://www.webopedia.com/TERM/A/application.html>
[2]See [37] Open projects software: Software definition,
<http://www.openprojects.org/software-definition.htm>
[3]See [50] Holey, Thomas, et al: Wirtschaftsinformatik, 2007, p. 279

2.1.2.2   Office applications

Office applications[4] refer to applications used to support office activities for word processing, spreadsheet calculations, preparation of presentation slides, graphic arts and database processing. There exist in the market several office applications such as Microsoft office, Lotus Smart Suite, Star Office and Wordperfect Office. The most known application suite is Microsoft Office, which includes Microsoft Word, Excel, PowerPoint and Access. The applications work closely together allowing the easy interaction and object exchange among each other.

2.1.2.3   Project management

Project management applications[5] allow project managers and team members to keep track of any project from its conception to its launch. The software manages all the project related aspects including resource management, budget management, time management, task assignments, quality control, issue reports and documentation management. Project management software provides a centralized view to the whole project and gives more transparency to all involved team members.

2.1.2.4   Team collaboration

Team collaboration software[6] offers proper conditions for the support and coordination of work related tasks within the company or among different companies. Using team collaboration software, project teams can work together to solve common problems and achieve better and faster goals. The team members have the possibility to work in parallel independant of the time and location. Team collaboration software has gained ultimately more importance with the globalization, the internationalization and the geographical distances between teams within the companies.

Team collaboration software combines different office and communication software such as the tools already mentioned in 2.1.2.1 and 2.1.2.2 but also includes project management functions, such as team tasks and time management, shared calendars, real-time joint view of information as well as problem solving processes in teams.

2.1.2.5   Customer relationship management

Customer relationship management software[7] gives the company the tools required to manage customer information. This information is important in order to deliver the customers what they want, provide them the best customer service possible, cross-sell and up-sell more effectively, close deals, understand who the customer is

---

[4]See [43] Holey, Thomas, et al: Wirtschaftsinformatik, 2007, p. 272

[5]See [41] Project management software: Project management software definition, <http://www.projectmanagementsoftware.com>

[6]See [56] Holey, Thomas, et al: Wirtschaftsinformatik, 2007, p. 281

[7]See [45] Webopedia, IT Business Edge: Customer relationship management software, <http://www.webopedia.com/TERM/C/CRM.html>

and retain current customers. The customer relationship management software will collect, manage and link the customer information with the goal of optimizing the customer's interaction.

2.1.2.6 Procurement

Procurement software[8] supports the purchase automatization functions in the companies.

All the activities related to create and approve purchase orders, select and order any product or service, receive and match an invoice and pay a bill are handled electronically and can be analyzed separately. The procurement department benefits of the information's centralization as it is possible to see what was ordered, ensure the needed approvals are available and compare current prices to get the best deal for the company.

2.1.2.7 Web development

Web development software[9] relates to software applications used to facilitate the design, implementation and deployment of a company's internet website, applications and web services. This type of software consists of a programming-oriented set of tools for linking web pages to databases and for manipulating other software components. A HTML editor for web development is included generally.

2.1.2.8 Unified messaging

Unified messaging software[10] is used to improve the communication within the company, accelerate and improve the quality of decisions based on real-time information, improve operational effectiveness and reduce travel and expenses cost. The main components of a unified messaging software are instant messaging, fax, email, web conferencing, real-time collaboration, presence and telephony integration.

2.1.2.9 Enterprise resource planning

Enterprise resource planning software[11] allows the companies to use a system of integrated applications to manage the business by integrating all aspects of the company's value chain including development, manufacturing, logistics, sales and marketing. Specifically, the enterprise resource planning software consists of different enterprise software modules, each one is focused on a specific area of the business

---

[8]See [55] Holey, Thomas, et al: Wirtschaftsinformatik, 2007, p. 287
[9]See [40] PC magazine encyclopedia: Web development software,
<http://www.pcmag.com/encyclopedia>
[10]See [34] IBM corporation: Unified communications,
<http://www-142.ibm.com/software/products/us/en/category/SWAAA>
[11]See [46] Webopedia, IT Business Edge: Enterprise Resource Planning software,
<http://www.webopedia.com/TERM/E/ERP.html>

process. The most common modules include those for product planning, material purchasing, inventory control, sales, accounting, marketing, finance and HR. The most important goal of the enterprise resource planning software is to provide one central repository for all information that is shared by all business processes in order to improve the flow of data across the company.

2.1.2.10 Fleet management

Fleet management software[12] is used for managing all the aspects and operations related to a fleet of vehicles operated by a company. Among the main functions of fleet management software are to manage all the processes, tasks and events such as notification of routine maintenance, scheduled maintenance, warranty tracking, work scheduling, depreciation, expense tracking, work order, parts inventory management and operational cost tracking.

2.1.2.11 Human resource

Human resource software[13] is used to support the human resource activities of the companies. The main functions of this software is to provide support in the recruitment process, payroll, time repoint, benefit administration, learning and training management, performance record, scheduling and absence management.

2.2 Fundamentals of cloud computing

2.2.1 Definition and characteristics

The term cloud computing refers to the possibility to execute any kind of process using a server connected to the internet. It is possible to upload and download documents, videos or pictures, which is commonly known as online storage. Cloud computing facilitates as well the execution of computer programs without having them installed at the own machines as the software is executed from supplier's servers connected to internet.

There are many definitions available to describe the term cloud computing. One simple definition[14] refers to cloud computing as the delivery of computing services without owning an own infrastructure.

Other entities define cloud computing as follows:

---

[12]See [51] Wikipedia: Fleet management software,
<http://en.wikipedia.org/wiki/Fleet_management_software>
[13]See [53] Wikipedia: Human resource management system,
<http://en.wikipedia.org/wiki/Human_resource_management_system>
[14]See [10] Metzger, Christian, et al: Cloud computing Chancen und Risiken aus technischer und unternehmerischer Sicht, 2011, p. 2

- NIST[15] defines cloud computing as a model for enabling ubiquitous, convenient, on-demand network access to a shared pool of configurable computing resources (e.g. networks, servers, storage, applications, and services) that can be rapidly provisioned and released with minimal management effort or service provider interaction. This cloud model is composed of five essential characteristics (on-demand self-service, broad network access, resource pooling, rapid elasticity, measured service), three service models (cloud software as a service (SaaS), cloud platform as a service (PaaS), cloud infrastructure as a service (IaaS)) and four deployment models (private cloud, community cloud, public cloud, hybrid cloud).

- Gartner[16] considers cloud computing as a style of computing where massively scalable IT-related capabilities are provided "as a service" across the internet to multiple external customers.

- Forrester[17] sees cloud computing as a pool of abstracted, highly scalable, and managed infrastructure capable of hosting end-customer applications and billed by consumption.

- T-Systems, a german IT consulting company, defines cloud computing[18] [19] [20] as the renting of infrastructure and software, as well as bandwidths, under defined service conditions. These components should be able to be adjusted daily to the needs of the customer and offered with the upmost availability and security. Included in cloud computing are end-to-end service level agreements (SLAs) and use-dependent service invoices.

Other definitions and aspects of cloud computing can be found in the following bibliographic references[21] [22] [23] [24] [25]:

In general terms, cloud computing refers to offer solutions and applications to the end users without a need for installation and deployment in the own end user premises. A cloud computing service can be software as a service, which delivers the entire application. In the infrastructure as a service model[26], only the servers and operating systems are provided, and customers deploy their own applications on the hardware.

---

[15]See [36] National Institute of Standards and Technology: NIST Definition of Cloud Computing, <http://csrc.nist.gov/publications/nistpubs/800-145/SP800-145.pdf>, pp. 2-3

[16]See [29] Gartner research: Gartner says cloud computing will be as influential as E-business, <http://www.gartner.com/it/page.jsp?id=707508>

[17]See [27] Forrester Research: Cloud computing definition, <http://www.forrester.com/rb/research>

[18]See [16] T-Systems Enterprise Services, White Paper. Cloud Computing I, 2011

[19]See [17] T-Systems Enterprise Services, White Paper. Cloud Computing II, 2011

[20]See [18] T-Systems Enterprise Services, White Paper. Dynamic Services, 2011

[21]See [19] Van Zütphen, Thomas: Avancen aus der Wolke, 2011

[22]See [15] Terplan, Kornel; Voigt, Christian: Cloud Computing, 2011

[23]See [21] Velte, Anthony, et al: Cloud computing: A practical approach, 2010

[24]See [1] Baun, Christian; Kunze, Marcel: Cloud computing: Web-basierte dynamische IT-Services, 2010

[25]See [20] Van Zütphen, Thomas: Der CIO als Cloud-Broker, 2011

[26]See [39] PC magazine encyclopedia: Definition of cloud computing, 2012

Section 2.2.3 will explain in detail the existing cloud computing service models. The cloud computing model is characterized by the benefits offered to the companies in terms of productivity, cost and flexibility. Cloud computing is seen as a trend with high potential to dominate the IT market due to the many advantages offered compared to current IT technologies. Nowadays, companies are forced to increase productivity, improve the cost structure and react faster to the changing market. By using cloud computing, companies benefit of the flexibility, scalability, price efficiency and mobility that can be reached with this service model.

Gartner research[27] estimates the cloud services revenue reached 68.3 US billion in 2010. Looking at the future, Gartner estimates the industry will strongly growth and reach a revenue of about 148.8 million by 2014.

2.2.2 Computer topology evolution

Over the last years, the computer topology moved from a monolithic and centralized environment based on mainframes to a distributed environments based on the client-server model. Recently, mesh environments are gaining importance. The mesh connectivity allows each system to communicate directly to others increasing the redundancy within the system. As a result, the data processing and storage may be shared between them in a dynamic manner. Figure 2.1[28] shows the computer topology evolution stages.

2.2.2.1 Mainframe

Mainframe computers[29] were introduced in the 1960s and consisted of centralized servers, which were deployed at customer's premises. This technology consisted of high available and performance computer systems that were very expensive and complex. Mainframes used normally the star network topology. This topology consists of computers connected directly to a mainframe.

Mainframes[30] were initially designed for big companies requiring the processing of high amount of information and data. Mainframes were scalable systems and connected to high-speed disk subsystems.

---

[27]See [28] Gartner research: Gartner Says Worldwide Cloud Services Market to Surpass $68 Billion in 2010, <http://www.gartner.com/it/page.jsp?id=1389313>

[28]See [14] Rhoton, John: Cloud Computing Explained, 2010, p. 31

[29]See [52] Wikipedia: Grossrechner, <http://de.wikipedia.org/wiki/Grossrechner, 2012>

[30]See [47] Webopedia, IT Business Edge: What is mainframe?, <http://www.webopedia.com/TERM/M/mainframe.html>

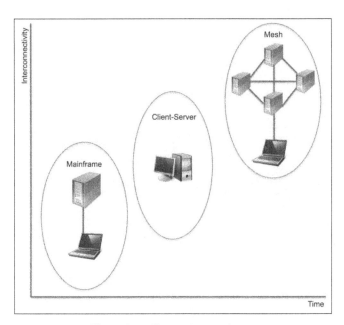

Figure 2.1: Connectivity evolution

2.2.2.2 Client-Server

The client-server model[31] introduced the possibility for a service requesters (also called client) to send tasks or workloads into a network for the further processing by service receivers (also called server). The servers receiving the requests process the information themselves or send it further to other computers connected to the network.

The servers in the client-server architecture[32] have high capacity and high performance for computing processing. This architecture provides a higher availability than the mainframe model as the clients are not only connected to one single server and in case of failover of one server, any other server connected to the network can process the information. The client-server model started to be used in the 1980s as applications were migrated from mainframes to networks of desktop computers.

2.2.2.3 Mesh topology

Finally, with the popularization of internet in the 1990s, the technology has seen an increased trend into the mesh connectivity. The mesh connectivity[33] allows that each

---

[31]See [48] Wikipedia: Client-server model,
<http://en.wikipedia.org/wiki/Client-server_model>
[32]See [38] PC magazine encyclopedia: Definition of client/server,
<http://www.pcmag.com/encyclopedia>
[33]See [14] Rhoton, John: Cloud Computing Explained, 2010, pp. 30-31

computer on the network can communicate to each other. Data processing, storage or any other computer process required can be dynamically shared and executed between systems. This model is highly scalable as the processes can be executed by distributed servers. Cloud computing bases on the mesh connectivity model. Figure 2.2[34] summarizes the computer topology evolution and presents the main characteristics.

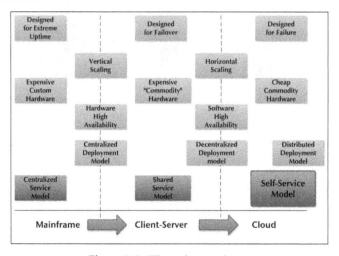

Figure 2.2: IT topology evolution

---
[34]See: [24] Bias, Randy: Debunking the "No Such Thing as A Private Cloud" Myth,
<http://www.cloudscaling.com/blog/cloud-computing/debunking-the-no-such-thing-as-a-private-cloud-myth/>

2.2.3   Cloud computing service models

With the introduction of cloud computing, companies perceive the deployment of infrastructure and software applications in a different way. There is not longer a need to invest high amount of money buying expensive and redundant systems or purchasing a high number of software licenses.

Several services models are identified in cloud computing covering from infrastructure and database virtualization to user applications. As of today, three cloud computing service models are identified in the literature as the most relevant:

- Infrastructure as a service
- Platform as a service
- Software as a service

The most know payment model is the pay-as-you-go-model (PAYG)[35].

Figure 2.3[36] shows some applications for each cloud computing service model, which will be described in more detail in the following sections 2.2.3.1, 2.2.3.2 and 2.2.3.3.

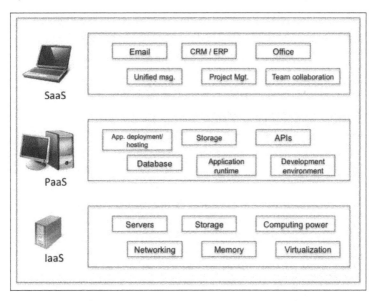

Figure 2.3: Cloud computing service models

---

[35]See [36] National Institute of Standards and Technology: NIST Definition of Cloud Computing, <http://csrc.nist.gov/publications/nistpubs/800-145/SP800-145.pdf>, 2011, pp. 2-3

[36]See [14] Rhoton, J.: Cloud Computing Explained, 2010, p. 22

2.2.3.1   Infrastructure as a Service

Infrastructure as a Service (IaaS)[37] operates at the lowest service level and refers to features including infrastructure like server, network, storage, memory and other computer related resources. Companies do not need to invest high amount of money purchasing, maintaining and operating an IT infrastructure as the complete infrastructure is operated and maintained by the cloud computing supplier. Additionally, companies can deploy any operating system and execute any application required. Cloud computing suppliers use the economies of scale by reducing the complexity of deploying a customer-specific infrastructure. Instead of this, a pool of servers and other infrastructure resources are setup and are made available to the companies. The term infrastructure as a service is also known as virtualization. Figure 2.4[38] presents some different types of IaaS services.

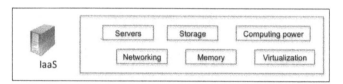

Figure 2.4: Infrastructure as a service stack

2.2.3.2   Platform as a Service

Platform as a Service model (PaaS)[39] operates at a higher level than infrastructure as a service. The platform as a service model provides the resources needed to develop, build, deploy, execute and maintain applications from the internet without the need to install the software in the own servers.

PaaS services include application design, development, testing, deployment and hosting. Figure 2.5[40] describes some further possible services applicable to PaaS.

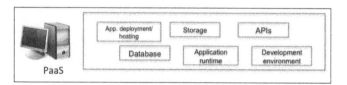

Figure 2.5: Platform as a service stack

---

[37]See [14] Rhoton, John: Cloud Computing Explained, 2010
[38]See [14] Rhoton, John: Cloud Computing Explained, 2010, pp. 13-14
[39]See [21] Velte , Anthony, et al: Cloud computing: a practical approach, 2010, p. 13
[40]See [14] Rhoton, John: Cloud Computing Explained, 2010, pp. 13-14

By adopting the PaaS service model[41], companies do not need to manage or control the underlying cloud infrastructure including network, servers, operating systems or storage, but they can still control the deployed applications and modify the configuration settings for the application-hosting environment.

2.2.3.3 Software as a Service

Software as a Service (SaaS)[42] is the most known and widest cloud computing service model used currently for the companies and people around the world. This model offers to customers business functionalities using the internet as enabler. Companies can use any software without installation at the own premises, without paying excessive and unnecessary license costs and without worrying about update installation and maintenance. The application can be accessed via internet using normally a web browser and independently of operating system or device used.
Figure 2.6[43] presents some applications covered by the SaaS model.

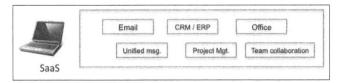

Figure 2.6: Software as a service stack

2.2.4 Advantages and limitations of cloud computing

2.2.4.1 Advantages of cloud computing

Adoption of cloud computing services brings many advantages for the companies[44]. The most important advantages of using cloud computing are described below:

- Possibility for the company to concentrate on core business
- There is not need for the company to invest resources in getting IT knowledge as the supplier brings its own expertise and specialized personal
- State-of-the-art solutions including infrastructure and software applications are always available as well as automatic updates
- Anywhere and anytime access independent of the device, computer or terminal used

---

[41]See [36] National Institute of Standards and Technology: NIST Definition of Cloud Computing, 2011, pp. 2-3
[42]See [21] Velte , Anthony, et al: Cloud computing: A practical approach, 2010, pp. 13-14
[43]See [14] Rhoton, John: Cloud Computing Explained, 2010, pp. 13-14
[44]See [10] Metzger, Christian, et all: Cloud computing, Chancen und Risiken aus technischer und unternehmerischer Sicht, 2011, p. 38f

- Reduction in the time to market due to factors such as the access to the latest technology
- High number of possible suppliers offers possibilities to reduce costs
- Economical advantages as there is no need for initial investment cost, reduction of operational cost and maintenance cost
- Cost efficiency is reached because the users of cloud computing only pay for the real service usage
- Multi-Tenancy plays an important economical aspect in terms of economies of scale. Adopting cloud computing services, users can share the same computing resources and there is not need to deploy a dedicated system for a unique user
- System scalability is one of the most important advantages of using cloud computing services. In case extra licenses or more servers are required, solution can be easily adapted to company's needs
- High system availability as agreed in service level agreements (SLAs) due to supplier's high performance systems
- Higher innovation potential by the use of state-of-the-art infrastructure, platforms and software. Companies benefit from the automatic updates performed directly from the suppliers
- Professional support by cloud computing supplier compared to small company.

2.2.4.2 Limitations of cloud computing

Following limitations[45] should be considered when adopting cloud computing services:

- Data security is considered the most important limitation and barrier factor for companies adopting cloud computing services. There are many constraints related to the security of information
- Correct functionality of infrastructure and software applications are highly dependent to internet access' availability and speed
- Companies implementing cloud computing services do not have the possibility to build up their own IT competence
- Adoption of cloud computing services adds high dependencies to supplier.

2.3   Fundamentals of success factors

2.3.1 Definition and characteristics

Success factors analysis[46] provides a set of variables with information where companies need to focus their resources and capabilities in order to succeed and gain

---

[45]See [10] Metzger, Christian, et all: Cloud computing, Chancen und Risiken aus technischer und unternehmerischer Sicht, 2011, p. 38f
[46]See [4] Grant, Robert: Contemporary strategy analysis, 2002, p. 100

competitive advantage in the market. The term success factor was defined initially by Chuck Hofer and Dan Schendel. They defined success factors[47] as "those variables that management can influence through its decisions and that can affect significantly the overall competitive positions of the firms in an industry. Within any particular industry they are derived from the interaction of two sets of variables, namely, the economic and technological characteristics of the industry and the competitive weapons on which the various firms in the industry have built their strategies".

Having knowledge of those success factors is not a guarantee for superior profitability but a good starting point to understand the industry environment and plan an effective business strategy[48], which will be used to allocate correctly the resources and capabilities in order to reach industry success.

Different studies[49] have been performed in order to provide empirical evidence of which business strategies lead to success and what are the key success factors. One of the most known studies is the profit impact of marketing strategy (PIMS) research program. The empirical investigation identified several strategic aspects that influence profitability. Among the most important strategic factors studied were market share, product quality, order of market entry and capital intensity. One of the most important results states the strategic factors are highly correlated with the profitability.

2.3.2 Methods to identify success factors

Based on Robert Grant's approach, two important aspects need to be considered for a company to succeed: The first aspect refers to knowing the customers and delivering them products they are willing to buy (see section 2.3.2.1). The second aspect consists of having a very good knowledge of the competition and its complex environment (see section 2.3.2.2). Figure 2.7[50] shows a basic framework introduced by Robert Grant which is used to identify key success factors.

2.3.2.1 Analysis of demand

The process of analysis of demand consists mainly in identifying who are the customers, what are their needs and what are the decision criteria they use to choose a particular product and company[51]. Once the factors have been identified, further analysis needs to be performed. For example, if customer's choice of software applications is based primarily in the data security and this is connected to the location

---

[47]See [5] Hofer, Chuck; Schendel, Dan: Strategy formulation: Analytical concepts, 1977, p. 77

[48]See [4]Grant, Robert, Contemporary strategy analysis, 2002, p. 100

[49]See [2] Buzzel, Robert: The PIMS program of strategy research. A retrospective appraisal, 2004

[50]See [4] p. 97

[51]See [4] p. 97

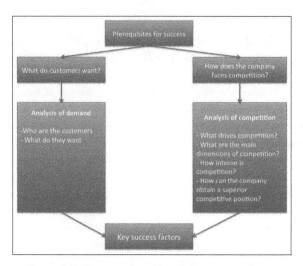

Figure 2.7: Framework to identify key success factors

of the servers, options related to server location offshore or in-customer-premises should be included into the offer by a cloud computing supplier.

Finally, Robert Grant refers in his book about the importance for a company to consider a customer not as a source of bargaining power but as a source of profit and as the main goal for the company's existence.

2.3.2.2 Analysis of competition

The second process consists on analyzing the current competition's situation in the industry[52]: how intense is the competition and what are its key dimensions. In the software market, consumers choose mainly the suppliers on the basis of market leadership and interoperability to existing systems. To reach this position, companies need to invest sufficiently enough resources in marketing advertising and product development.

2.4   Fundamentals of small- and medium-sized businesses

2.4.1 Definition and characteristics

Small- and medium-sized businesses play a very important social and economical role in many countries around the world[53]. As an example, 99% of the companies in the european union are represented by small- and medium-sized businesses. They provide around 90 million jobs and contribute to entrepreneurship and innovation.

---

[52]See [4] Grant, Robert, Contemporary strategy analysis, 2002, p. 97
[53]See [3] European Union: Commission recommendation concerning the definition of micro, small and medium-sized enterprises, 2003

The categorization of small- and medium-sized businesses is made based on the employees headcount and the revenues. The employees headcount is an initial criterion for determining in which category an small- and medium-sized business is located. It covers full-time, part-time and seasonal employes. The revenues is the second aspect to consider and it is determined by calculating the income that a company received during a year from its sales and services.

In general terms, small- and medium-sized businesses characterize for employing fewer than 250 persons and for having revenues not exceeding 50 million euro.

Typically, small-and medium-sized businesses are export-oriented, focus on innovative and high value manufactured products and have a worldwide domination of a niche market. They are typically privately owned and based in small rural communities. Many of the successful small-and medium-sized companies characterize for a long-term oriented approach with the adoption of modern management practices, like focusing on employee satisfaction, implementation of lean manufacturing practices and total quality management.

2.4.2 Definition of small- and medium-sized businesses

2.4.2.1 Small-sized businesses

Small-sized businesses are defined as companies employing fewer than 50 persons and with revenues not exceeding 10 million euro[54].

2.4.2.2 Medium-sized businesses

Medium-sized businesses consist of companies which employ fewer than 250 persons and which have revenues not exceeding 50 million euro[55].

---

[54]See [3] European Union: Commission recommendation concerning the definition of micro, small and medium-sized enterprises, 2003

[55]See [3]

CHAPTER 3

State-of-the-art research

This section presents some studies available in the literature, which focus on the adoption of cloud computing services at different companies including specially small- and medium-sized businesses.

3.1 Cloud computing in the insurance industry

A first investigation analyzed in scope of this master thesis was the study performed by Fraunhofer - Institute for work management and organization[1] which investigated the role of cloud computing in the insurance market. This study was part of the research program THESEUS sponsored by the german economical and technological ministry.

The overall investigation consisted of two surveys. The first study was directed to the insurance companies and the second one to IT suppliers in the insurance market. In total, 15 insurance companies and 27 IT suppliers participated in the research. The small- and medium-sized companies in the insurance sector were represented by 4 insurance companies and 17 IT suppliers. The main goal of this research was to identify the potential adoption of cloud computing for this particular sector and the benefits and challenges of cloud computing services in the insurance market.

In general, the awareness level for topics related to cloud computing services is very high in insurance companies and their IT suppliers. From the supplier's side, a high interest for including cloud computing services in their portfolio was identified and one fifth of the suppliers are already offering cloud computing services. From user's point of view, the interest to adopt cloud computing services is very low: few insurance companies are currently using cloud computing services or even planning its use. In order to support the spreading of cloud computing technologies, a high effort directed to the companies, in form of guidance and consultancy, is required. Companies in the insurance market need to understand better the benefits and risks of adopting cloud computing services.

In regards to the key success factors, the topic security has a high relevance. Insurance companies as well as IT suppliers have many concerns to topics related to security. For that reason, it is important to focus on providing secure cloud computing technologies based on the state-of-the-art technologies in terms of security.

---

[1]See [23] Weidmann, Monika; Renner, Thomas; Rex, Sascha: Cloud computing in der Versicherungsbranche, 2010

Other important factors such as transparency from supplier's side and good communication, as well compliance to security standards and independently performed security audits play an important role. Another important aspect consists in making sure that a smooth integration and compatibility of the new cloud computing services into the existing systems is possible.

3.2 Cloud computing in the logistics sector

A second study in the area of cloud computing was performed by Fraunhofer-Institute for software and system techniques titled cloud computing for small- and medium-sized businesses in the logistics sector[2]. The focus of this investigation was to identify barriers for the adoption of cloud computing services and provide recommendations to cloud computing suppliers in order to overcome them.

In general, 60% of the decision makers in the logistics sector have plans to adopt cloud computing services and have a basic understanding of this new technology. The study refers as well to the key role of the cost saving factor. Logistic companies agreed in considering the cost transparency offered by adopting cloud services as an important factor as well the wide possibilities to track the costs and look continuously for improvements.

In regards to the relevant factors, companies consider there is a deficit in the information provided about cloud computing benefits, which can be solved with information campaigns which include best practice- and real use cases of cloud computing services working currently in different companies. The companies in the logistics sector consider: "the cloud computing technology might be there but there is not measurable and concrete facts based on the deployments available"[3]. A further important factor to consider relates to the interoperability to existing systems as well as the possibility to customize the solutions and integrate them with third-party solutions. Last but not least, the data security and the trust to the cloud computing supplier are considered by the logistic companies as important.

---

[2]See [9] Holtkamp, Berndhard: Cloud Computing für den Mittelstand am Beispiel der Logistikbranche, 2010
[3]See [9] p. 19

CHAPTER 4

Empirical survey

4.1 Objective

The empirical investigation done in scope of this master thesis was performed in cooperation with the cloud computing business unit of Deutsche Telekom and had the main goal to identify the most relevant cloud computing solutions, which are planned to be adopted by small- and medium-sized businesses. The investigation helped as well to identify the level of acceptance and current usage of cloud computing services in small- and medium-sized businesses.

Another aspect investigated consists in identifying the most relevant aspects for the adoption of solutions based on the cloud computing model. Those aspects were used to identify the key success factors needed for the adoption of cloud computing services. Companies planning to adopt cloud computing based services were in focus. The empirical investigation includes 15 factors, which are important for a successful adoption of cloud computing services. These factors are organized in six different groups: security-, cost-, technology-, support- and supplier-related factors.

The empirical research investigates different aspects of cloud computing with the main focus on following questions:

- Is your company interested in using cloud computing services?
- Does your company already use cloud computing services?
- What cloud computing service model is currently being used at your company? What service model is planned to be used?
- What is the most relevant software as a service application your company is planning to use?
- What kind of service provider is your company using for the applications currently working?
- What are the most important aspects to consider when your company would plan to adopt a cloud computing service?

By identifying the most significant cloud computing applications and those key success factors relevant for the adoption of cloud computing services, it shall be feasible for a cloud computing supplier to effectively offer the specific applications fulfilling the necessary requirements.

4.2   Method

The empirical investigation consists of an online survey with a participation of 613
employees working as IT decision makers in different industry sectors. The employees represent companies with a number of employees ranging from 1 to 249. Based
on the definition for small-and medium-sized businesses as described in section 2.4.2,
companies were segmented as follows: 432 companies fulfilled the requirements of
small-sized businesses, 148 companies were identified as medium-sized companies.
33 of the companies interviewed could not be categorized in the small- and medium-
sized businesses as they did not fulfill the requisites in terms of revenues. In total,
580 companies were identified as small- and medium-sized businesses and the empirical investigation done in scope of this master thesis based on this figure.
The industries included in the investigation were:

- IT and technology
- Professional services
- Consultancy
- Retail
- Financial services
- Building industry
- Law, audit
- Media, publishing
- Healthcare
- Electronics
- Automotive
- Logistics
- Mechanical engineering
- Telecommunications

The participants were asked about the current applications being used at their
companies, about the acceptance of cloud services, the plans to include cloud services
in the company, the requirements and barriers to be considered for the adoption of
cloud computing services. The survey had a duration of around 15 minutes and was
performed in the dates from 13th to 23rd of December 2011. The most relevant
questions for this master thesis are included in the appendix A in the page 63.

4.3   Sample

This section provides the most important information about the small- and medium-sized companies participating in the empirical research. Aspects like the industry distribution, the number of employees and the revenues are described in the following sections.

4.3.1   Industry distribution

Figures 4.1 and 4.2 show the industry distribution of the small- and medium-sized companies, which have participated in the survey.

For the small-sized companies segment, companies representing technology, professional services, consultancy and retail branches cover 49% of the companies interviewed. The total number of small-sized businesses is 432.

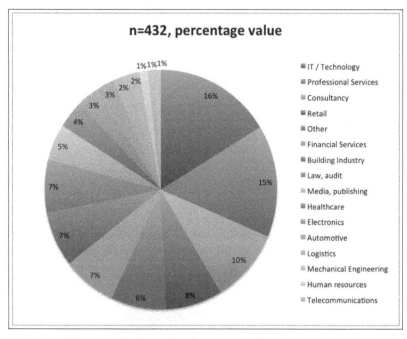

Figure 4.1: Industry distribution in small-sized companies

The medium-sized companies are dominated by companies working in the area of technology, mechanical engineering, professional services, retail, building industry and electronics (59%). 148 medium-sized companies have participated in this survey.

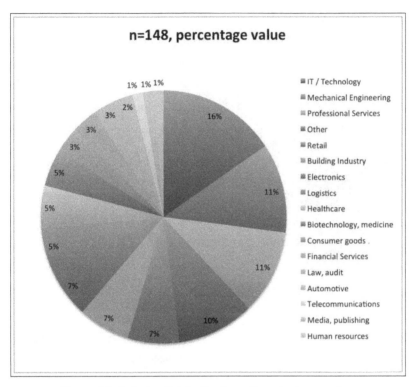

Figure 4.2: Industry distribution in medium-sized companies

4.3.2 Employees distribution

From the small-sized businesses, companies with fewer than 5 employees represented 58% of the interviewed companies as shown in the figure 4.3.

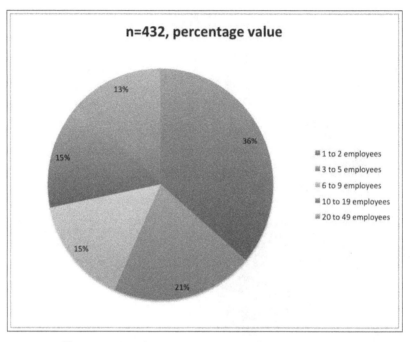

Figure 4.3: Number of employees in small-sized companies

In figure 4.4 it can be identified, the medium-sized business group is dominated by companies with a number of employees ranging from 50 to 250 and representing 90% of the interviewed companies.

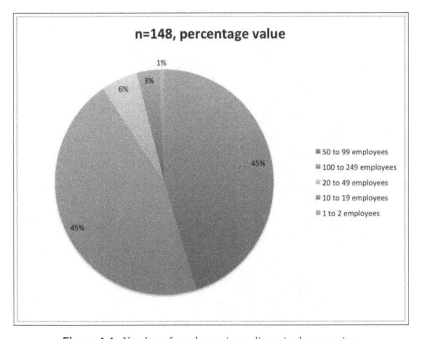

Figure 4.4: Number of employees in medium-sized companies

4.3.3 Revenues distribution

Revenues for small-sized companies have in a range from less than 500 thousand euro to 10 million euro. The figure 4.5 shows that a high percent of the small-sized companies (58%) has revenues below 500 thousand euro.

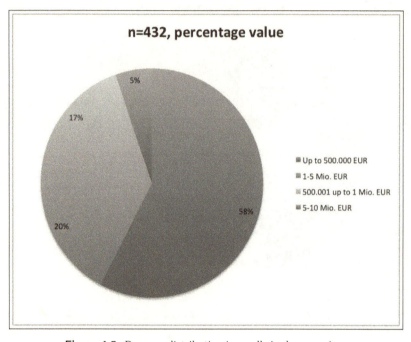

Figure 4.5: Revenue distribution in small-sized companies

In the case of medium-sized businesses, 71% of the companies has revenues ranging between 5 and 50 million euro. Figure 4.6 shows the whole distribution of medium-size businesses based on the revenues.

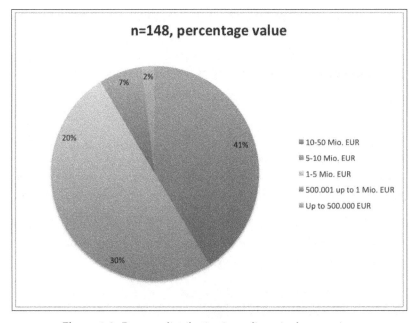

Figure 4.6: Revenue distribution in medium-sized companies

CHAPTER 5

Analysis of cloud computing applications for small- and medium-sized businesses

5.1 Acceptance and usage of cloud computing

5.1.1 Acceptance of cloud computing

The empirical investigation based on the online survey as presented in section 4.2 shows similar results of cloud computing acceptance for small- and medium-sized businesses. Basically, companies have a neutral position in terms of implementing cloud computing services in a short-term. 36% of the small-sized businesses neither reject the use of cloud computing services nor plan the use yet. Similar results are available for medium-sized business with 34% located in this segment.

Unexpectedly, there is a high tendency in small- and medium-sized businesses for not considering the use of cloud computing services. 36% of small and 27% of medium-sized businesses consider the use of cloud computing services as an irrelevant topic for the companies.

Results also exhibit a lack of knowledge for cloud computing topics as 11% of the small-sized businesses hear about the new technology for the first time. Companies belonging to the medium-sized businesses group have more knowledge about cloud computing technologies and the term cloud computing is new for only 5% of them. On the other hand, 10% of the small-sized businesses plan to use cloud services in the near future compared to 23% of the medium-sized group. It can also be identified that 7% of the small-sized businesses and 11% of the medium-sized businesses are using cloud services already. Figure 5.1 and figure 5.2 present the complete results in term of acceptance of cloud services.

In general, there is a higher acceptance for cloud computing services in medium-sized businesses and a significant lack of knowledge in small-sized businesses. Based on this information, a need to educate and increase the awareness in small-sized business in terms of cloud computing was identified.

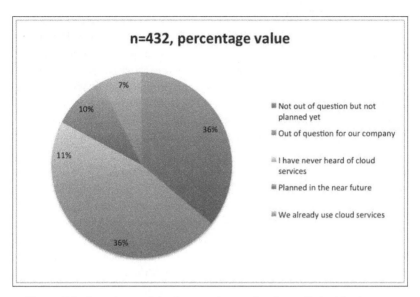

Figure 5.1: Acceptance of cloud computing services in small-sized businesses

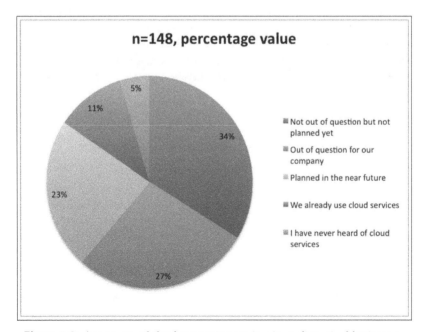

Figure 5.2: Acceptance of cloud computing services in medium-sized businesses

5.1.2 Usage of cloud services models

Based on the results of cloud computing acceptance previously presented, the usage of each cloud computing service model was also questioned. The focus now is to identify the current use and the plans for using any of the cloud computing service models. Only the companies showing either an interest in cloud computing service or already using them have been asked. Companies rejecting the usage of cloud computing services were out of scope. In total, 230 out of 432 small-sized companies have shown interest in cloud computing services and 100 out of 148 of the medium-sized companies.

From the results it can be identified small- and medium-sized businesses have a special interest in the software as a service model. 42% of the small-sized businesses are planning to use the software as a service model and 8% already used it. In the medium-sized business group, 53% are planning to use a software as a service application and 16% are already using one.

Infrastructure as a service represents the second most relevant cloud computing service model: 39% of small-sized businesses and 47% of the medium-sized businesses are considering to use infrastructure as a service as an alternative to the traditional model.

Finally, the platform as a service model appears to be the least relevant as 63% of the small-sized companies and 51% of the medium-sized companies are not planning to use a solution based on this model. The results surprisingly show a current use of platform as a service in medium-sized businesses. 13% of the medium-sized businesses are currently using the platform as a service model contrarily to small-sized businesses using the model only 4% of the companies. Results are shown in the figures 5.3 and 5.4.

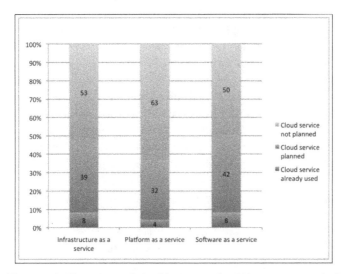

Figure 5.3: Usage in small-sized businesses (n=230, percentage value)

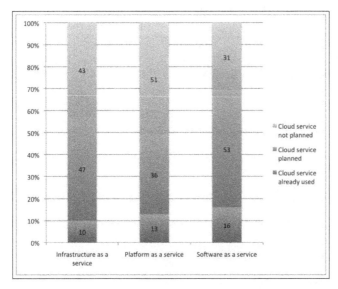

Figure 5.4: Usage in medium-sized businesses (n=100, percentage value)

Summarizing the survey's results in terms of acceptance and usage, there is a general interest in the small-and medium-sized companies to adopt cloud computing services and cloud computing technologies are well accepted in the industry, however a lack of information for topics related to cloud computing was identified. It is worth to mention, when companies were asked about the cloud computing definition, employees of small- and medium-sized companies frequently connected the term cloud computing to the new cloud services, which are being promoted recently by Apple and Deutsche Telekom such as iCloud and TelekomCloud.

There is still a big gap to be filled with consultancy and intensive information sessions as part of a business development strategy to accelerate the decision process at the companies. The consultancy should concentrate on informing the companies about the immense opportunities and advantages by adopting cloud computing services, as well as the limitations and constraints and the different alternatives to overcome them.

Finally, the empirical investigation shows software as a service solution is the cloud computing service with the highest acceptance among the small- and medium-sized companies. The next sections will present the results in terms of cloud computing services with a main focus on software as a service applications as this cloud computing model is gaining high importance within companies.

In addition, marketplaces are becoming more known and a new option for the companies. The term marketplace[1] is used in cloud computing terminology to describe a unique place where companies can find a collection of cloud computing applications. Currently, there is a small selection of marketplaces available which include the marketplace from Salesforce[2] and the Google Marketplace[3].

Specifically for the german market there is an initiative called "initiative cloud services made in Germany "[4] with the purpose of centralizing the cloud computing applications .

5.2 Cloud computing solutions

5.2.1 Infrastructure as a service solution

Infrastructure as a service is an interesting option for small- and medium-sized companies willing to use virtual servers for data processing and storage instead of operating their own servers.

---

[1]See [30] Göldie, Andreas: Google macht Ernst mit Cloud Computing, <http://netzwertig.com/2010/03/11/app-marketplace-google-macht-ernst-mit-enterprise-cloud-computing>

[2]See [42] Salesforce: The cloud computing marketplace from Salesforce, <http://appexchange.salesforce.com/home>

[3]See [32] Google: Google Apps Marketplace, <http://www.google.com/enterprise/marketplace>

[4]See [33] Grohmann, Werner: Initiative Cloud Services Made in Germany, <http://www.cloud-services-made-in-germany.de>

The adoption of the infrastructure as a service model brings many benefits to the companies: there is no need for purchasing any server infrastructure as the servers are located remotely in the supplier's premises. Companies benefit from the scalability and system dimensioning of the systems and the lower operational, administrative and maintenance cost compared to the traditional method.

There are however some limitations to consider when adopting infrastructure as a service solution like the dependance on the internet availability and speed and the potential integration costs to the infrastructure currently available.

The next sections present the results of the empirical investigation covering the infrastructure as a service model. The number of companies using infrastructure as a service solutions is low based on the survey: 19 small-sized businesses and 10 medium-sized businesses.

5.2.1.1   Storage

Storage refers to a supplier renting storage capacity to end users[5]. The storage service has gained importance due to the increased complexity of backup, replication and disaster recovery at the companies, especially in small- and medium-sized companies.

The empirical investigation shows similar results for the current usage of storage in small- and medium-sized businesses. Figure 5.5 and 5.6 show that the infrastructure as a service model is dominated by the storage service as 89% of the small- and 80% of the medium-sized businesses are using the service.

5.2.1.2   Processing / Computing power

The term processing or computing power refers to the possibility to rent servers for performing computational processes.

The figures 5.5 and 5.6 show the usage of processing power services in medium-sized companies of 20% compared to 5% at small-sized companies.

In general terms, the infrastructure as a service model plays an insignificant role as cloud computing model. In case an adoption is planned, storage as a service needs to be considered as interesting solution for small- and medium-sized businesses.

---

[5]See [21] Velte , Anthony, et al: Cloud computing: A practical approach, 2010, p. 136

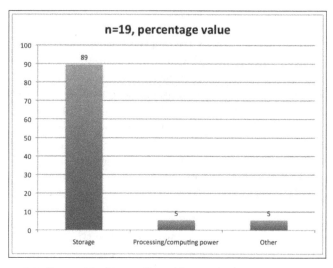

Figure 5.5: Usage of IaaS in small-sized businesses (n=19, percentage value)

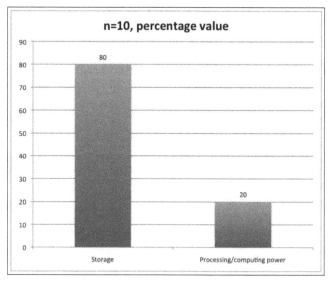

Figure 5.6: Usage of IaaS in medium-sized businesses (n=10, percentage value)

5.2.2   Platform as a Service solution

Platform as a service has a relevance for companies building their own applications and hosting them without purchasing a development platform or a hosting server as they are located at the cloud supplier's side. Using platform as a service solutions, companies benefit from renting the state-of-the-art development platform available, increasing also the time to market and avoiding high initial cost. Some limitations like the new dependencies to the cloud supplier or some initial effort required in the customization need to be considered.

Following sections summarize the results of the empirical investigation.

5.2.2.1   Application deployment and hosting

The application deployment and hosting service enables users to deploy and run applications remotely using the cloud suppliers infrastructure. Despite the low number of companies currently using platform as a service solutions (10 small-sized businesses and 13 medium-sized businesses, the result shows a tendency at small- and medium-sized businesses of using application deployment and hosting service as shown in the figures 5.7 (50% of the small-sized companies) and figure 5.8 (69% of the medium-sized companies). Specifically, the service Microsoft Azure was mentioned several times when asked about the platform as a service model.

5.2.2.2   Storage

The storage service refers to the possibility to store and manage the own applications on the cloud supplier servers. Companies benefit of the backup and redundancy functionalities of the cloud computing supplier. The storage service is the second most used platform as a service model and has more relevance in small-sized businesses (40%) than in medium-sized businesses (8%).

5.2.2.3   Development environment

The development environment allows companies to develop, build and run applications. Normally the platform as a service include an operating system and developer tools. This solution has a low significance in small-sized businesses with a usage of 10%. At the other side, it has a higher relevance for medium-sized businesses as 23% of the interviewed companies are using this solution.

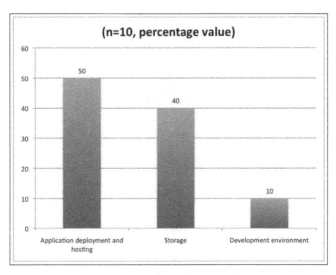

Figure 5.7: Usage of PaaS in small-sized businesses (n=10, percentage value)

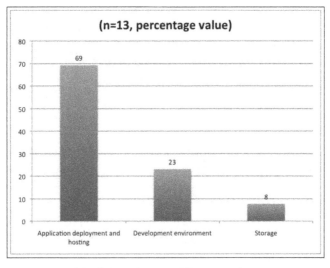

Figure 5.8: Usage of PaaS in medium-sized businesses (n=13, percentage value)

5.2.3   Software as a Service solution

The software as a service segment is the most known and prevalent cloud computing service used in the industry. Apart from the general cloud computing advantages, companies benefit from the cost transparency and cost reduction, the easy scalability, high availability and the possibility for device independent access of the software. Despite of this, the security of the company's information represents the key constraint for the adoption of software as a service applications.

The following sections show the results of the empirical investigation, which was presented in section 4.2. The results provide information about the type of software as a service application planned to be adopted in the companies. Figure 5.9 and 5.10 present the results of the survey. In total, 107 small-sized businesses and 67 medium-sized businesses use applications based on cloud computing model.

It is important to identify the current software application supplier as the switching cost play a key role for the adoption of a new system. As defined by Michael Porter[6], switching costs are fixed cost that buyers face when they change supplier. Such costs may arise because a buyer switching a vendor must, for example, alter product specifications, train employees to use the new system, or modify processes or information systems. Information about the current suppliers preference is briefly discussed and discussed in this section.

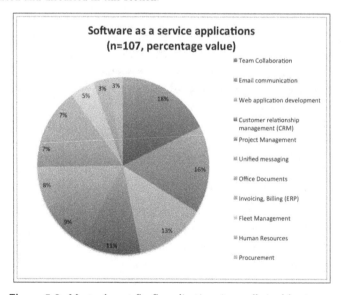

Figure 5.9: Most relevant SaaS applications in small-sized businesses

---

[6]See [13] Porter, Michael E.: The five competitive forces that shape strategy, 2008, p. 4

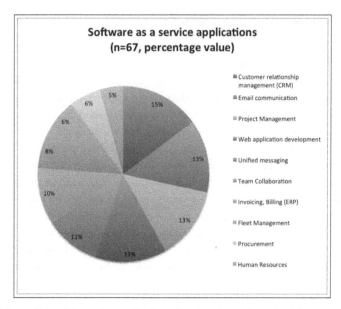

Figure 5.10: Most relevant SaaS applications in medium-sized businesses

5.2.3.1   Team collaboration

As described in section 2.1.2.4, team collaboration software refers to centralized document sharing platforms for easy access from team members.

Team collaboration applications represent the first position of preference for software as as service applications among small-sized companies. 18% of the small-sized businesses are planning to adopt team collaboration applications as a software as a service compared to 10% of the medium-sized businesses.

Regarding the top providers for team collaboration applications, Dropbox and Microsoft Sharepoint are used in many of the companies interviewed.

5.2.3.2   Email communication

Email communication refers to applications for use of email services (see section 2.1.2.1). Email communication as software as a service has an important relevancy in the small-and medium-sized companies and is positioned at the second place of preference for small- and medium-sized business with 16% and 13% respectively.

It was identified, the email communication software market is clearly dominated by Microsoft Outlook.

5.2.3.3   Web development

Web development software refers to applications for development of internet websites (see further definition in section 2.1.2.7).

Web development software has an increasing importance and there is a high level of acceptance of adopting the software as a service model. 13% of small-sized businesses and 13% of the medium-sized businesses plan to adopt the model in short-term.

The web development software market is shared between two companies, Adobe and Microsoft with the products Adobe Dreamweaver and Microsoft WebMatrix.

5.2.3.4   Customer relationship management

Customer relationship management tools are used to manage customer information and use it in order to improve the customer interaction (see section 2.1.2.5). Customer relationship management as software as a service has a very high relevance in medium-sized businesses and locates in the first place of relevance with 15% of the companies planning to shift to the cloud computing model. In terms of small-sized businesses, the software has a moderate 11% of relevance.

Currently, small-and medium-sized businesses are using traditional software from two main suppliers, Microsoft Dynamics and SAP CRM.

5.2.3.5   Project management

Project management software is used in companies for all activities related to coordination of projects (see section 2.1.2.3). The usage of project management software as cloud service is different for small- and medium-sized businesses. While the cloud computing service is relevant for medium-sized businesses with 13% of relevance and locating in the second place of preference, the service was selected by 9% of the small-sized companies.

With respect to the current usage, Microsoft Project dominates clearly the market and most of the companies are using the stand-alone software.

5.2.3.6   Unified messaging

Unified messaging software is used for improving the communication within the company and consists of a set of applications such as instant messaging, web conferencing and presence (refer to section 2.1.2.8).

The empirical investigation exhibits similar results for small- and medium-sized businesses and positions the software as a service model for unified messing in a medium significance level. Only 8% and 11% of the small- and medium-sized businesses are planning to adopt the cloud computing model.

Concerning the stand-alone solutions currently deployed in the companies, the market is shared among Skype and Microsoft Lync.

5.2.3.7 Office documents

The office document software segment applies to applications used for word processing, spreadsheet calculations, preparation of slides and database processing (refer to section 2.1.2.2).

Surprisingly, the relevance of office document software based on software as a service is not well accepted and companies are not planning to move the current application into the new technology. Only 7% of the small-sized businesses are considering the use of this new model. Medium-sized businesses are not planning the shift at all as none (0%) of the companies are planning to adopt the cloud model.

Regarding the market share of current office document software used, Microsoft Office dominates clearly the market.

5.2.3.8 Enterprise resource planning

Enterprise resource planning software is used to centralize and manage the aspects related to the value chain of a company (see section 2.1.2.9).

The adoption of this type of software as software as a service is not well accepted. Only 7% of the small-sized businesses and 8% of the small-sized business are planning to adopt the cloud model. Companies stated as main reason for the low usage data security concerns.

The market of stand-alone applications in small-and medium-sized businesses is dominated by Lexware and SAP.

5.2.3.9 Fleet management

As described in section 2.1.2.10, fleet management software is used for managing the aspects related to a fleet of vehicles.

Fleet management based on the software as a service model has a very low significance with only 5% and 6% of the small- and medium-sized businesses planning to use the cloud model, respectively.

The market of stand-alone software for fleet management in small-and medium-sized businesses in Germany is dominated mainly by german companies such as Lexware and WISO.

5.2.3.10 Human resource management

Human resource management software supports the activities related to management of employee information (refer to section 2.1.2.11).

This type of software has a low relevance and the plans for adopting the application as cloud model are very low. 3% of small- and 5% of medium-sized companies have plans to shift the existing applications into the new technology.

The current market share of stand-alone applications in small-and medium-sized businesses is divided between Lexware and SAP.

Summarizing, the most relevant applications most likely to be adopted by small-sized businesses based on the empirical investigation are:

- Software for team collaboration, email communication and web development play a key role and have the highest possibility to be adopted by small-sized companies at short-term
- The second group of relevance consists of software applications for customer relationship management, project management and unified messaging
- Finally, software applications in the area of office documentation, enterprise resource planning, fleet management, human resources and procurement have currently an insignificant role.

Concerning the adoption of cloud computing applications at medium-sized businesses based on the software as a service model, the empirical investigation shows the following results:

- Customer Relationship Management, email communication, project management and web development have the first place in relevance
- A second group of relevance consists of software applications for unified messaging, team collaboration and enterprise resource planning
- Software applications related to fleet management, procurement and human resources have the least level of significance.

CHAPTER 6

Analysis of success factors for cloud computing for small- and medium-sized businesses

6.1 Security related factors

6.1.1 Overview

This section evaluates the importance of security-related factors in small- and medium-sized businesses as determinant for the adoption of cloud computing services. Security related factors consist of three factors such as data security, data storage in Germany and security audits. The research results are presented in the figures 6.1 and 6.2.The number of companies, which selected security related factors, consists of 216 small-sized businesses and 117 medium-sized businesses.

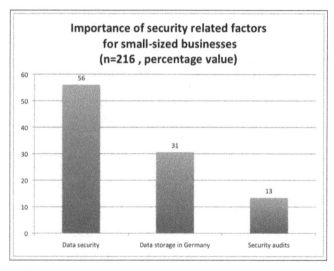

Figure 6.1: Security related factors for small-sized businesses

6.1.2 Data security

A high number of companies participating in the empirical investigation consider the data security as a very important factor. The results for small- and medium-sized

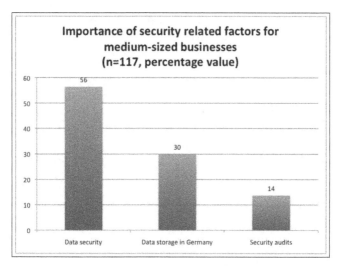

Figure 6.2: Security related factors for medium-sized businesses

business are identical. 56% of the companies placed data security as the first factor of importance concerning security.

The importance of data security is very well understood by cloud computing suppliers and is identified as one of the main constraints for the adoption of cloud computing solutions by companies. For this reason, cloud computing suppliers need to increase the transparency in terms of information regarding security aspects by including details in their offers such as the compliance to existing industry security standards (ISO 27001, EU model clauses, etc.). Additionally, the available policies, the different layers of security used, the proactive and continuos data monitoring in order to identify potential malicious access and the access restriction to production servers facilitate as well a high transparency.

6.1.3 Data storage in Germany

Companies interviewed consider the data location as an essential factor. Cloud computing suppliers shall offer guarantees about data storage in the local country, in this case, Germany, as the empirical research was directed uniquely to companies located in Germany. The adoption of cloud computing services in small- and medium-sized businesses relates not only to the data storage in Germany but also to provide transparent information about who has access to the information.

6.1.4 Security audits

Unexpectedly, the results of the empirical investigation show the lowest values for the factors related to security audits. Companies are not expecting regular controls from certified organization such as TÜV and see this aspect as the least important. This result has a relevancy for the cloud computing suppliers and can rely on the fact, that companies consider the credibility and transparency from cloud computing suppliers as an essential factor.

6.2 Cost related factors

6.2.1 Overview

Cost-related factors play an essential role as a factor for adopting cloud solutions and is considered as one of the most important benefits for using cloud computing services.

This section evaluates the importance of cost-related factors in small- and medium-sized businesses by analyzing following factors: low cost and cost transparency.

Figures 6.3 and 6.4 present the results for the cost-related factors for 191 small-sized businesses and 105 medium-sized businesses.

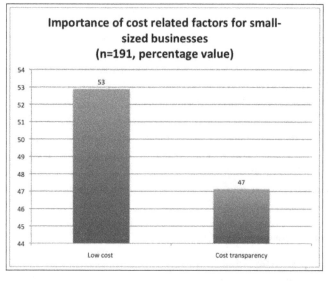

Figure 6.3: Cost related factors for small-sized businesses

6.2.2 Low cost

Cost savings translated to aspects such as low initial investment, low operational cost and low maintenance cost are key decision factors for small- and medium-sized businesses planning to adopt cloud computing services. Companies benefit from the economies of scale in term of technology solutions offered by cloud computing

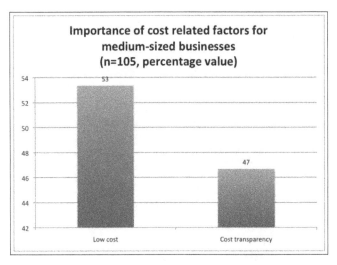

Figure 6.4: Cost related factors for medium-sized businesses

suppliers. The results of the survey show similar values for the group of companies interviewed: 53% relevance for small-sized businesses and 53% relevance for medium-sized businesses.

It is important to mention, companies planning to use cloud computing services are familiar with the benefits of cloud computing in terms of cost savings and they consider this factor as one of the key advantages of this technology.

6.2.3 Price transparency

Price or cost transparency has a remarkable position as a cost factor for the adoption of cloud computing services and are very high rated in the empirical investigation's results. Companies consider important to be able to track and understand the actual cost of the used solutions. Cloud services makes feasible to track the actual cost as the services base on the pay-as-you-go billing model.

6.3   Technology related factors

6.3.1   Overview

The questions related to technology related factors show slightly different results. In general, service stability and interoperability to existing systems are considered as the most relevant factors for small- and medium-sized businesses. Features related to customization have lower importance in small-sized businesses, fomented by factors like cost savings as a result of the economies of scale achieved with cloud computing. Those factors were identified and presented in the previous section as main focus for companies adopting cloud computing services and particularly in the early stages of implementation.

Results related to technology related factors are presented in figure 6.5 and figure 6.6 for 196 small-sized businesses and 101 medium-sized businesses, which considered technology related factors as important.

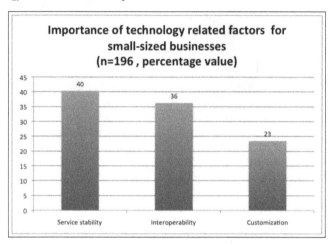

Figure 6.5: Technology related factors for small-sized businesses

6.3.2 Service stability

The service stability factor has a slightly higher relevance for small-sized businesses than for medium-sized businesses, however the factor is located in the first two places of importance in terms of technology for both groups: 40% of small-sized businesses considered the factor as relevant compared to 32% of medium-sized businesses. Smooth functionality must be guaranteed and a stable and reliable framework around the cloud services must be available. Factors like stability and speed of the internet connection are additional variables not present in stand-alone solutions. Cloud computing suppliers need to cooperate with internet providers in order to guarantee high availability and superior internet connection to the adopters of cloud computing services.

6.3.3 Interoperability

Interoperability to existing systems has a higher importance for medium-sized businesses. A reason may be related to the existence of a more established infrastructure in medium-sized business compared to small-sized businesses, which results also in more concerns regarding interoperability and migration costs: higher interoperability efforts lead to higher migration costs. These costs will have an impact on the

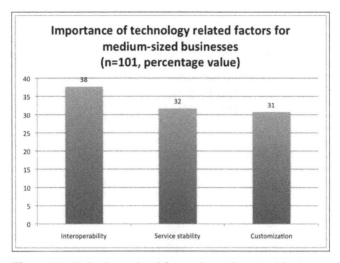

Figure 6.6: Technology related factors for medium-sized businesses

cloud computing adoption decision. Adoption of cloud computing services will success whether a smooth interoperability to existing systems is guaranteed. The factor interoperability was selected by 36% of small-sized businesses and 38% of medium-sized businesses as relevant.

6.3.4 Customization

The economies of scale and the effects in the possibilities of customization are well understood by small-sized companies. The customization factor plays an insignificant role for this group (23%).

In terms of medium-sized businesses, the relatively high relevance might be connected to a more advanced, complex and specialized infrastructure (31%).

6.4 Support related factors

6.4.1 Overview

The relevance of support related factors is similar for small-and medium-sized businesses based on the empirical investigation. A permanent support via phone and email preferably in german language is expected. As a result of the new technologies and the wide internet usage, cloud computing suppliers can guarantee this permanent support.

On-site support is considered by around one third of the small-and medium-sized businesses as important, followed by support in the setup and migration.

A summary of the factors is shown in the figures 6.7 and 6.8 for 137 small-sized businesses and 82 medium-sized businesses.

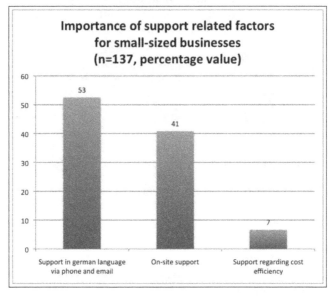

Figure 6.7: Support related factors for small-sized businesses

6.4.2   Support in german language via phone and email

A contact person for support in case of difficulties in the form of a hotline or email plays a key role for the adoption of cloud computing services. It is very important for the cloud computing suppliers to guarantee this support to the small-and medium sized businesses in questions facing the whole adoption process such as planning, setting-up, deployment and execution of the cloud computing services. The support shall be preferably in german language. The factor was selected by more than half of the companies: 53% of small-sized businesses and 51% of medium-sized businesses.

6.4.3   On-site support

On-site support has the second place of relevance and is mainly needed during the implementation phase when the cloud computing solutions must be integrated to the current company's infrastructure.

On-site support is connected to the presence of the company in the local country, in this case, the company having the headquarter or a subsidiary in Germany. 41% of the small-sized businesses and 40% of the medium-sized businesses considered the on-site support as important.

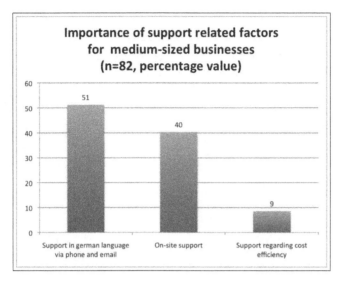

Figure 6.8: Support related factors for medium-sized businesses

6.4.4 Support regarding cost efficiency

The last position within the support related factors consists of support in early stages of the adoption process. Cost reduction needs to be verifiable and an offer around answering questions related to the verification of cost saving needs to be available. This verification can be supported with methods such as the total cost of ownership method.

6.5 Supplier related factors

6.5.1 Overview

None of the analyzed factors delivered such different results in terms of significance as the supplier related factors. However, the factors were equally distributed and each one represents approximately one forth of the overall results.

Figures 6.9 and 6.10 exhibit the empirical results for supplier related factors for 109 small-sized businesses and 69 medium-sized businesses.

6.5.2 Headquarter in Germany

Small-and medium-sized businesses agreed about the importance of the origin of the cloud computing supplier and the preference of selecting a supplier with headquarters in Germany. Not only a big german company is preferred but also a regional partner. The empirical investigation gives information about the very low preference of small-

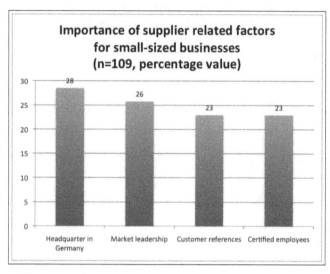

Figure 6.9: Supplier related factors for small-sized businesses

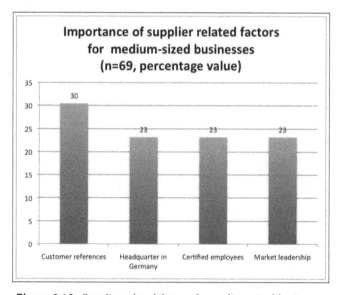

Figure 6.10: Supplier related factors for medium-sized businesses

and medium-sized companies for selecting foreign cloud suppliers specially from the USA, which is a result of the low reputation they have in terms of security in Germany. 28% of small-sized businesses and 23% of medium-sized businesses consider a cloud computing supplier with headquarter in Germany as important.

6.5.3 Customer references

The factor related to customer references has a more important role for medium-sized (30%) than for small-sized businesses (23%) occupying the first place of relevance. Medium-sized businesses expect from the cloud computing suppliers an already gained reputation and trust with respect to other companies and specially with the DAX companies. Customer references include a wide range of aspects as for example professionalism, customer service and exactitude to fulfill deadlines and budget estimations.

6.5.4 Certified employees

The aspect of cloud computing suppliers having employees holding original equipment certifications is not seen as a relevant factor neither for small-sized nor for medium-sized companies. This can be related to other factors, which have more importance such as trust to the cloud computing supplier.

6.5.5 Market leadership

Market leadership has a slightly more relevance for small-sized businesses than for medium-sized businesses. In general terms, the factor is not relevant at all as the empirical investigation reveals the importance of some other factors when the adoption of cloud computing services is planned.

Summarizing, the most relevant factors concerning the adoption of cloud computing services in small-and medium sized businesses based on the empirical investigation are:

- The aspect concerning data security occupies the first place of relevance and it is considered a critical factor influencing the decision to adopt the cloud computing service
- Companies understand the benefits of cloud computing in terms of cost transparency and the lower cost compared to stand-alone solutions. The cost saving related factors are well accepted by the companies
- Despite the high advances in terms of technology, companies have concerns regarding new dependencies which are added in the adoption of cloud computing technologies such as dependencies to the internet availability and internet speed

- The empirical results exhibit the importance of permanent support to accompany the small- and medium-sized companies during the whole adoption process including preferably support in german language
- There is a high tendency to prefer local suppliers with good references of previous cloud computing deliveries.

CHAPTER 7

Conclusions

Services based on the cloud computing model are gaining more and more importance
and in a short-term, they are planned to change considerably the way, companies are
managing currently their IT resources. Nowadays, companies are facing a increased
and more complexed number of challenges and the need to overcome them in shorter
time and with limited financial and personal resources are getting more relevant to
success in the industry.

The adoption of cloud computing brings many possibilities to the current organization in terms of adapt the scalability, optimization of resource allocation, cost
flexibility, use of state-of-the-art technologies and faster time-to-market.

The empirical investigation performed in the scope of this master thesis and the
available research analyzed exhibit similar results. The adoption of cloud computing technologies is well accepted and there is a high interest to adopt solutions based
on cloud computing in small- and medium-sized businesses.

In terms of cloud computing solutions, the software as a service solution was identified as the cloud computing service with the most acceptance in the small- and
medium-sized companies, followed by the infrastructure as a service model.

Regarding the preference for software as a service applications, it was identified by
the survey, small- and medium-sized businesses have plans to adopt cloud computing
applications in areas for improving the communication within the companies and
the employees' mobility such as team collaboration and unified messaging solutions,
as well as supporting the daily work such as project management and email communication solutions. Applications involving sensitive company's and customer's
information such as enterprise resource planning, procurement and human resource
applications have the least preference and the short-term adoption is not planned.

When focusing on key success factors, security related factors represents an important concern for companies planning to adopt cloud computing services. Small- and
medium-sized companies expect from cloud computing suppliers transparency and
credibility with the handling of information. Cost saving and cost transparency ob-

tained with the adoption of cloud computing services have also high importance in small-and medium-sized companies. The benefits of economy of scale and possibility to concentrate on the core business are well accepted in the companies analyzed. Further factors identified in the scope of the empirical investigation are concerns related to the internet connection as a new enabler for cloud computing applications, the requirements in terms of support in the local language and the preference for local suppliers.

Additionally, the empirical investigation identified a general lack of information about topics concerning best practices for the adoption of cloud computing services including also the evaluation of adoption costs and risks. This gap in terms of information can be filled with professional consultancy and intensive information sessions as part of a business development strategy in order to accelerate the decision process in the companies. The importance of this aspect is already understood by some cloud computing suppliers, which affirmed, the sales effort is spent, most of the time, providing consultancy to the potential cloud computing adopters.

Online survey

A.1 Screening

A.1.1 Frage S1

Zu welcher der folgenden Branchen gehört das Unternehmen, in dem Sie tätig sind?
Bitte zutreffende Antwort anklicken.

1. Automobil
2. Konsumgüterhersteller
3. Finanzdienstleistungen
4. Rechts- und Steuerberatung, Wirtschaftsprüfung
5. Professionelle Dienstleistungen
6. IT / Technologie
7. Handel
8. Telekommunikation
9. Logistik und Verkehr
10. Gesundheitswesen
11. Bauwirtschaft
12. Biotechnologie, Chemie, Pharmazie und Medizin
13. Elektronik, Elektrotechnik, Technik
14. Maschinen- und Anlagenbau
15. Medien, Verlag, Druck
16. Personaldienstleistungen, Arbeitsvermittlung
17. Unternehmensberatung

A.1.2 Frage S2

In welchem Ausmaß sind Sie in Ihrem Unternehmen an Entscheidungen über die
EDV/IT beteiligt? Bitte zutreffende Antwort anklicken.

1. Ich bin der Hauptentscheider / einer der Hauptentscheider, wenn es um solche
   Technologien geht
2. Ich bin Mitentscheider, wenn es um solche Technologien geht
3. Ich nehme bei solchen Technologien keinen Einfluss auf die Entscheidung

A.1.3 Frage S9

Wie viele Mitarbeiter, Sie eingeschlossen, sind in Ihrem Unternehmen beschäftigt? Bitte zutreffende Antwort anklicken. Wenn nicht genau bekannt, bitte schätzen.

1. bis 2 Mitarbeiter
2. 3 bis 5 Mitarbeiter
3. 6 bis 9 Mitarbeiter
4. 10 bis 19 Mitarbeiter
5. 20 bis 49 Mitarbeiter
6. 50 bis 99 Mitarbeiter
7. 100 bis 249 Mitarbeiter

A.1.4 Frage S11

Wie hoch ist der Jahresumsatz Ihres Unternehmens? Bitte zutreffende Antwort anklicken. Wenn nicht genau bekannt, bitte schätzen.

1. Unter 500.000 EUR
2. 500.001 EUR bis 1 Mio. EUR
3. Über 1 Mio. EUR, aber weniger als 5 Mio. EUR
4. Über 5 Mio. EUR, aber weniger als 10 Mio. EUR
5. Über 10 Mio. EUR, aber weniger als 50 Mio. EUR
6. Über 50 Mio. EUR, aber weniger als 100 Mio. EUR
7. Über 100 Mio. EUR, aber weniger als 250 Mio. EUR
8. Über 250 Mio. EUR

A.2 Derzeitige Ausstattung an EDV/IT-Lösungen

A.2.1 Frage G5

Welche Art von EDV/IT Anwendungen setzen Sie in Ihrem Unternehmen ein? Anwendungen für... Bitte alle zutreffenden Antworten anklicken.

1. E-Mail Kommunikation (z.B. Microsoft Outlook, IBM Lotus, Apple Mail)
2. Unified Messaging wie Fax, Chat, Telefonie aus EDV/IT-Lösung, keine herkömmliche Telefonanlage (z.B. Microsoft Lync, IBM Lotus, Google, OpenScape)
3. Textbearbeitung, Tabellenkalkulation und Präsentationen (z.B. Microsoft Office, Google Docs, Lotus, OpenOffice)
4. Projektmanagement (z.B. Microsoft Project, SAP, Primavera, OpenProj)
5. Teamzusammenarbeit (z.B. Microsoft Sharepoint, Skype, Dropbox)
6. Kundenkontaktmanagement bzw. die Kundenpflege - CRM (z.B. Microsoft Navision, SAP, Oracle Siebel, Salesforce)
7. Betriebswirtschaftliche Belange, wie Rechnungserstellung, Warenwirtschaft oder Finanzbuchhaltung - ERP (z.B. SAP, Oracle, Microsoft, Lexware, WISO)

8. Personalwesen, wie Lohnbuchhaltung, Zeiterfassung etc. (z.b. SAP, Microsoft Dynamics, Oracle)

9. Mobile Aussendienstunterstützung, wie Vertriebsunterstützung, Flottenmanagement etc. (z.b. SAP, Lexware)

10. Anwendungen zur Unterstützung des Einkaufsprozesses (z.b. SAP, Onventis)

11. Web Applications Development (z.b. Adobe Dreamweaver, Microsoft WebMatrix, Google)

12. Sonstiges, und zwar ...

A.2.2 Frage G6/1a, Filter: Frage G5 Pos. 1 (E-Mail Kommunikation) geklickt

Sie haben angegeben, dass Sie Anwendungen für E-Mail Kommunikation nutzen. Welches der folgenden Softwareprodukte nutzen Sie dabei? Bitte zutreffende Antworte anklicken.

1. Microsoft Outlook
2. IBM Lotus Notes
3. Thunderbird
4. KMail
5. Opera
6. Pegasus Mail
7. (Apple) Mail
8. Eudora
9. Google Mail
10. Sonstiges, und zwar ...

A.2.3 Frage G6/2a, Filter: Frage G5 Pos. 2 (Unified Messaging) geklickt

Sie haben angegeben, dass Sie Anwendungen für Unified Messaging nutzen. Welche der folgenden Anwendungen nutzen Sie dabei genau? Bitte zutreffende Antwort anklicken.

1. IBM Lotus Sametime
2. IBM Lotus Domino
3. Microsoft Exchange Server
4. Microsoft Communications Server
5. Microsoft Lync
6. Octopus Desk Unified Communications (Deutsche Telekom)
7. OneBox
8. Google Dienste
9. Aastra
10. OmniTouch (Alcatel-Lucent)

11. Avaya Aura
12. OpenScape (Siemens Enterprise Communication und Microsoft)
13. Cisco Unified Products
14. NEC Univerge Lösung
15. 3COM Unified Messaging
16. Hewlett-Packard Unified Communication and Collaboration-Messaging
17. Nortel CallPilot
18. Oracle Communications Unified Communications
19. Panasonic Unified Communications
20. Interactive Intelligence
21. Mitel
22. Sonstige, und zwar ...

A.2.4 Frage G6/2b , Filter: Frage G5 Pos. 2 (Unified Messaging) geklickt

Welches Feature nutzen Ihre Mitarbeiter am meisten, wenn es um Unified Messaging geht? Bitte zutreffende Antwort anklicken.

1. Instant Messaging
2. Telephonie/VoIP
3. Email
4. Fax
5. Videokonferenz
6. Applikationsharing
7. Location
8. Sonstiges, und zwar ...

A.2.5 Frage G6/3a , Filter: Frage G5 Pos. 3 (Textbearbeitung, Tabellenkalkulation und Präsentationen) geklickt

Sie haben angegeben, dass Sie Anwendungen für Textbearbeitung, Tabellenkalkulation und Präsentationen nutzen. Welche Office-Anwendungen nutzen Sie genau? Bitte zutreffende Antwort anklicken.

1. Microsoft Office
2. Microsoft Works
3. Google Docs
4. Lotus Symphony
5. Lotus SmartSuite
6. StarOffice (Sun)
7. Corel WordPerfect
8. OxygenOffice Professional
9. ZoHo

10. OpenOffice
11. LibreOffice
12. Sonstiges, und zwar ...

A.2.6 Frage G6/4a , Filter: Frage G5 Pos. 4 (Projektmanagement) geklickt

Sie haben angegeben, dass Sie Anwendungen für Projektmanagement nutzen. Welche der folgenden Anwendungen nutzen Sie genau? Bitte zutreffende Antwort anklicken.

1. Microsoft Project
2. SAP RPM
3. Primavera Project Planner
4. OpenProj
5. InLoox
6. Cando
7. Clocking IT
8. Sonstiges, und zwar ...

A.2.7 Frage G6/5a , Filter: Frage G5 Pos. 5 (Teamzusammenarbeit) geklickt

Sie haben angegeben, dass Sie Anwendungen für Teamzusammenarbeit nutzen. Welche der folgenden Anwendungen nutzen Sie genau? Bitte zutreffende Antwort anklicken.

1. Microsoft Sharepoint
2. Google Docs
3. Skype
4. MSN
5. Dropbox
6. TeamBox
7. Staction
8. Zoho Projects
9. activeCollab
10. Klok
11. GroupMind
12. Colabolo
13. Novel GroupWise
14. WorkSpace
15. IBM lotus domino
16. Microsoft Exchange Server
17. Sonstige, und zwar ...

A.2.8   Frage G6/6a , Filter: Frage G5 Pos. 6 (Kundenkontaktmanagement bzw. Kundenpflege - CRM) geklickt

Sie haben angegeben, dass Sie Anwendungen für Kundenkontaktmanagement bzw. Kundenpflege (CRM) nutzen. Welche der folgenden Anwendungen nutzen Sie genau? Bitte zutreffende Antwort anklicken.

1. Microsoft Dynamics NAV
2. SAP CRM
3. Oracle Siebel
4. Salesforce.com
5. Cobra CRM
6. AMTANGEE CRM Software
7. Acabus Plus
8. MX-Contact
9. CAS PIA
10. AVE! Prodatis
11. Daylite
12. Eva/3
13. Sonstige, und zwar ...

A.2.9   Frage G6/7a , Filter: Frage G5 Pos. 7 (Betriebswirtschaftliche Belange) geklickt

Sie haben angegeben, dass Sie Anwendungen für betriebswirtschaftliche Belange wie Rechnungserstellung, Warenwirtschaft und Finanzbuchhaltung - ERP nutzen. Welche der folgenden Anwendungen nutzen Sie genau? Bitte zutreffende Antwort anklicken.

1. SAP
2. Oracle
3. Siebel
4. Microsoft Dynamics AX + NAV
5. SAS
6. Lexware
7. WISO
8. TZ-EasyBuch
9. PSI
10. Abas-Business-Software
11. AvERP
12. inforCOM
13. SAGE
14. Monkey Office

15. EAR 15
16. JobDISPO
17. proALPHA
18. APPlus
19. Epicor
20. SoftM
21. Sonstige, und zwar ...

A.2.10 Frage G6/8a, Filter: Frage G5 Pos. 8 (Personalwesen) geklickt

Sie haben angegeben, dass Sie Anwendungen für Personalwesen nutzen. Welche der folgenden Anwendungen zur Lohnbuchhaltung bzw. Zeiterfassung nutzen Sie genau? Bitte zutreffende Antwort anklicken.

1. SAP
2. Microsoft Dynamics NAV + AX
3. Oracle
4. Siebel
5. SAS
6. Adata Lohn und Gehalt
7. ADDISON
8. ACCENON
9. CHRONOS
10. FOCONIS
11. Lotus
12. LODAS
13. Lexware
14. ATOSS
15. AIDA
16. ARGOS
17. ZEBAU
18. PROMPT
19. Sonstige, und zwar...

A.2.11 Frage G6/9a, Filter: Frage G5 Pos. 9 (Aussendienstunterstützung) geklickt

Sie haben angegeben, dass Sie Anwendungen für mobile Aussendienstunterstützung nutzen. Welche der folgenden Anwendungen nutzen Sie genau? Bitte zutreffende Antwort anklicken.

1. Lexware
2. BüroWARE

3. FABIS

4. Tectura

5. WISO

6. KFZ

7. MonKey

8. Project2web

9. Colib

10. PROMPT

11. Sonstige, und zwar ...

A.2.12   Frage G6/10a, Filter: Frage G5 Pos. 10 (Unterstützung des Einkaufsprozesses) geklickt

Sie haben angegeben, dass Sie Anwendungen für Unterstützung des Einkaufsprozesses nutzen. Welche der folgenden Anwendungen nutzen Sie genau? Bitte zutreffende Antwort anklicken.

1. SAP

2. Onventis

3. Wallmedien

4. Ariba

5. Simple systems

6. CommerceOne

7. Business Mart

8. Pool4tool

9. JCatalog

10. Amicron

11. Lexware

12. Sage

13. Sonstige, und zwar ...

A.2.13   Frage G6/11a, Filter: Frage G5 Pos. 11 (Web Applications Development) geklickt

Sie haben angegeben, dass Sie Anwendungen für Web Applications Development nutzen. Welche der folgenden Anwendungen werden bereits in Ihrem Unternehmen genutzt? Bitte zutreffende Antwort anklicken.

1. Adobe Dreamweaver

2. Adobe Flash

3. Adobe

4. ColdFusion

5. Google

6. Microsoft WebMatrix
7. RapidWeaver
8. WaveMaker
9. ASP.NET
10. CFEclipse
11. Adobe
12. Zend Development
13. Cincom
14. WebORB
15. Sonstige, und zwar ...

A.2.14   Frage G7

Wie werden die Anwendung in Ihrem Unternehmen betrieben? Bitte jeweils zutreffende Antwort anklicken.

1. E-Mail Kommunikation (z.b. Microsoft Outlook, IBM Lotus, Apple Mail)
2. Unified Messaging wie Fax, Chat, Telefonie aus EDV/IT-Lösung, keine herkömmliche Telefonanlage (z.b. Microsoft Lync, IBM Lotus, Google, OpenScape)
3. Textbearbeitung, Tabellenkalkulation und Präsentationen (z.b. Microsoft Office, Google Docs, Lotus, OpenOffice)
4. Projektmanagement (z.b. Microsoft Project, SAP, Primavera, OpenProj)
5. Teamzusammenarbeit (z.b. Microsoft Sharepoint, Skype, Dropbox)
6. Kundenkontaktmanagement bzw. die Kundenpflege - CRM (z.b. Microsoft Navision, SAP, Oracle Siebel, Salesforce)
7. Betriebswirtschaftliche Belange, wie Rechnungserstellung, Warenwirtschaft oder Finanzbuchhaltung - ERP (z.b. SAP, Oracle, Microsoft, Lexware, WISO)
8. Personalwesen, wie Lohnbuchhaltung, Zeiterfassung etc. (z.b. SAP, Microsoft Dynamics, Oracle)
9. Mobile Aussendienstunterstützung, wie Vertriebsunterstützung, Flottenmanagement etc. (z.b. SAP, Lexware)
10. Anwendungen zur Unterstützung des Einkaufsprozesses (z.b. SAP, Onventis)
11. Web Applications Development (z.b. Adobe Dreamweaver, Microsoft WebMatrix, Google)
12. Sonstiges, und zwar...
    Antwortmöglichkeiten:
13. Installation auf dem Unternehmensserver mit Clients auf den PC/Notebooks der Mitarbeitern
14. Einzelinstallationen auf den PC/Notebooks der Mitarbeiter
15. Betrieb durch eine EDV/IT Dienstleister ausserhalb des Unternehmensnetzwerks
16. Software as a Service, Cloud Anbieter (z.b. Salesforce)

17. Sonstiges

A.2.15 Frage G8

Welche Art von Support wird von Ihrem jeweiligen Anbieter der verschiedenen Anwendungen angeboten? Bitte jeweils zutreffende Antwort anklicken.

1. E-Mail Kommunikation (z.B. Microsoft Outlook, IBM Lotus, Apple Mail)
2. Unified Messaging wie Fax, Chat, Telefonie aus EDV/IT-Lösung, keine herkömmliche Telefonanlage (z.B. Microsoft Lync, IBM Lotus, Google, OpenScape)
3. Textbearbeitung, Tabellenkalkulation und Präsentationen (z.B. Microsoft Office, Google Docs, Lotus, OpenOffice)
4. Projektmanagement (z.B. Microsoft Project, SAP, Primavera, OpenProj)
5. Teamzusammenarbeit (z.B. Microsoft Sharepoint, Skype, Dropbox)
6. Kundenkontaktmanagement bzw. die Kundenpflege - CRM (z.B. Microsoft Navision, SAP, Oracle Siebel, Salesforce)
7. Betriebswirtschaftliche Belange, wie Rechnungserstellung, Warenwirtschaft oder Finanzbuchhaltung - EHP (z.B. SAP, Oracle, Microsoft, Lexware, WISO)
8. Personalwesen, wie Lohnbuchhaltung, Zeiterfassung etc. (z.B. SAP, Microsoft Dynamics, Oracle)
9. Mobile Aussendienstunterstützung, wie Vertriebsunterstützung, Flottenmanagement etc. (z.B. SAP, Lexware)
10. Anwendungen zur Unterstützung des Einkaufsprozesses (z.B. SAP, Onventis)
11. Web Applications Development (z.B. Adobe Dreamweaver, Microsoft WebMatrix, Google)
12. Sonstiges, und zwar

A.2.15.1 Antwortmöglichkeiten:

1. Telefonisch
2. Vor-Ort
3. Remote
4. Sonstiges

A.2.16 Frage G10

Wie zufrieden sind Sie mit den derzeitigen EDV/IT Anwendungen insgesamt? Bitte zutreffende Antwort anklicken.

1. äusserst zufrieden
2. Sehr zufrieden
3. Zufrieden
4. Eher unzufrieden
5. Überhaupt nicht zufrieden

A.2.17   Frage G11, Filter: G10 Pos. 1-2

Warum sind Sie mit Ihren derzeitigen Anwendungen so zufrieden? Bitte schreiben Sie alles auf, was Ihnen hierzu einfällt. Bitte Antworten möglichst detailliert eingeben.

A.2.18   Frage G12, Filter: G10 Pos. 3-5

Warum sind Sie mit Ihren derzeitigen Anwendungen eher nicht zufrieden? Bitte schreiben Sie alles auf, was Ihnen hierzu einfällt. Bitte Antworten möglichst detailliert eingeben.

A.2.19   Frage G13

Könnten Sie sich vorstellen, Cloud-Services zu nutzen, damit sind bspw. Anwendungen gemeint, die nicht mehr bei Ihnen installiert sind, sondern von einem Anbieter bereitgestellt werden und über einen Internetanschluss erreichbar sind? Bitte zutreffende Antwort anklicken.

1. Ich habe noch nicht von einem Cloud Service gehört
2. Cloud Services kommt in unserem Unternehmen nicht in Frage
3. Cloud Services kommt in unserem Unternehmen in Frage, die Anschaffung ist aber nicht geplant
4. Die Anschaffung Cloud Services ist in nächster Zeit geplant
5. Wir nutzen Cloud Services bereits in unserem Unternehmen

A.2.20   Frage G14, Filter: Frage G13 Pos. 3-4 geklickt ("kommt in Frage"/ "in nächster Zeit geplant")

In welchem Zeitrahmen wird in Ihrem Unternehmen an die Einführung von Cloud Services gedacht? Bitte zutreffende Antwort anklicken.

1. Sofort
2. 1-3 Monate
3. 3-6 Monate
4. 6 Monate- 1 Jahr
5. 1 Jahr-2 Jahre
6. >2 Jahre

A.2.21   Frage G15 , Filter: Frage G13 Pos. 3-5 geklickt ("kommt in Frage"/ "in nächster Zeit geplant"/"wird bereits genutzt")

Welche Art von Cloud Services nutzen bzw. planen Sie zu nutzen? Bitte zutreffende Antwort anklicken.

1. SaaS - "Software as a Service"
2. PaaS - "Platform as a Service"

3. IaaS - "Infrastructure as a Service" (z.B Storage, Computing power)
4. Sonstiges, und zwar ...

Antwortmöglichkeiten:

1. Wird bereits genutzt
2. Nutzung ist geplant
3. Nutzung ist nicht geplant

A.2.22 Frage G16, Filter: Frage G15_1 Pos. 1-2 ("SaaS wird bereits genutzt", "Nutzung ist geplant")

Welche Art von "Software as a Service" planen Sie in nächster Zeit anzuschaffen? Bitte jeweils nach zutreffender Wichtigkeit anklicken.

1. E-Mail Kommunikation
2. Unified Messaging wie Fax, Chat, Telefonie
3. Textbearbeitung, Tabellenkalkulation und Präsentationen
4. Projektmanagement
5. Teamzusammenarbeit
6. Kundenkontaktmanagement bzw. die Kundenpflege - CRM
7. Betriebswirtschaftliche Belange, wie Rechnungserstellung, Warenwirtschaft oder Finanzbuchhaltung)
8. Personalwesen, wie Lohnbuchhaltung, Zeiterfassung etc.
9. Mobile Aussendienstunterstützung, wie Vertriebsunterstützung, Flottenmanagement etc.
10. Anwendungen zur Unterstützung des Einkaufsprozesses
11. Absicherung des Unternehmensnetzes wie Firewall, Intrusion Prevention, Antivirensoftware /E-Mail-Schutz
12. Sonstiges, und zwar ...

Antwortmöglichkeiten:

1. Am wichtigsten
2. Am zweitwichtigsten
3. Am drittwichtigsten
4. Am viertwichtigsten

A.2.23 Frage G21, Filter: Frage G15_3 Pos. 1 ("IaaS wird bereits genutzt")

Welche Art von IaaS - "Infrastructure as a Service" nutzen Sie? Bitte zutreffende Antwort anklicken.

1. Im Bereich Speicher (Storage)
2. Im Bereich Rechenleistung (Computing / processing power)
3. Sonstiges, und zwar ...

A.2.24   Frage G22, Filter: Frage G13 Pos. 3-5 geklickt ("kommt in Frage"/ "in nächster Zeit geplant"/ "wird bereits genutzt")

Bitte beschreiben Sie die Cloud Services näher, die für Sie in Frage kommen, die Sie nutzen bzw. planen? Bitte nennen Sie auch insbesondere den Anbieter. Bitte schreiben Sie alles auf, was Ihnen hierzu einfällt. Bitte Antworten möglichst detailliert eingeben.

A.2.25   Frage G23, Filter: Frage G13 Pos. 3-5 geklickt ("kommt in Frage"/ "in nächster Zeit geplant"/ "wird bereits genutzt")

Wer ist für Sie der ideale Anbieter für die zuvor beschriebenen Cloud Services? Bitte zutreffende Antwort anklicken.

1. Großer amerikanischer Anbieter
2. Großer deutscher Anbieter
3. über einen regionalen IT Partner /IT-Systemhaus
4. über einen überregionalen Anbieter
5. über den Anbieter der Branchensoftware
6. über einen IT-Händler/Distributor
7. Sonstiges, und zwar ...

A.2.26   Frage G24, Filter: Frage G13 Pos. 3-5 geklickt ("kommt in Frage""in nächster Zeit geplant""wird bereits genutzt")

Denken Sie dabei an einen bestimmten Anbieter? Würden Sie uns diesen bitte nennen? Bitte Antworten möglichst detailliert eingeben.

A.2.27   Frage G25, Filter: Frage G13 Pos. 3-4 geklickt ("kommt in Frage"/"in nächster Zeit geplant")

Welche der folgenden Aspekte wären Ihnen wichtig, wenn Sie nach einem Anbieter für Cloud Services suchen würden? Bitte wählen Sie die 5 wichtigsten Kriterien aus! Bitte zutreffende Antwort anklicken.

1. Marktführerschaft des Anbieters / Größe des Anbieters
2. Niedrige Kosten
3. Kostentransparenz
4. Datenstandort in Deutschland
5. Firmenhauptsitz in Deutschland
6. Sicherheitsaspekte
7. Verträge und SLA (Service Level Agreements) nach deutschen Recht
8. Deutschsprachigen Kundenservice (telefonisch, schriftlich)
9. Kundenservice in Deutschland (persönlich)

10. Regelmäßige Prüfung von Rechenzentrum und Ablaufprozesse durch zertifizierte Security-Auditors (z.b. TüV)
11. Zertifizierte Mitarbeiter
12. Kundenreferenzen
13. Anpassungsmöglichkeit / Kundenspezifisches Produkt
14. Support bei der Prüfung von Betriebskosten-Senkung
15. Unterstützung bei Einführung und Migration der Altsysteme
16. Kompatibilität der Anwendung zu bestehenden Systemen
17. Schulung
18. Sonstiges, und zwar...

A.2.28 Frage G26, Filter: Frage G13 Pos. 1-4 geklickt ("noch nichts von Cloud gehört"/"kommt nicht in Frage"/"kommt in Frage"/"in nächster Zeit geplant")

Was sind Ihrer Meinung nach die Hauptgründe, die gegen eine Einführung von Cloud Services sprechen könnten? Bitte wählen Sie die 5 wichtigsten Gründen aus! Bitte zutreffende Antwort anklicken.

1. Kein Mehrwert
2. Hohe Entwicklungsaufwand
3. Hohe Initialkosten
4. Hohe Migrationskosten
5. Sicherheitsbedenken
6. Geringe Verfügbarkeit von Mitarbeiter / IT Kompetenz nicht vorhanden
7. Geringe Kompatibilität mit bestehenden Systemen / Anwendungen
8. Geringes Vertrauen zu neue Technologien
9. Die notwendigen Investitionen wären zu hoch
10. Datenschutz bzw. -missbrauch
11. Datensicherheitsbedenken
12. IT-Kompetenzverlust
13. Geringe Verfügbarkeit und Netzgeschwindigkeit
14. Neue Abhängigkeit von Cloud-Anbietern
15. Proprietäre Lösungen
16. Kein Vertrauen in Cloud-Anwendungen
17. Fehlende Preis-Transparenz
18. Kostenentwicklung nicht planbar
19. Zuverlässigkeit des Internets
20. Sonstiges, und zwar ...

LIST OF FIGURES

LIST OF ABBREVIATIONS

CAD	Computer-aided design	NIST	National Institute of Standards and Technology
CC	Cloud Computing		
CRM	Customer Relationship Management	p.	Page
		Paas	Platform as a Service
DAX	German stock index (Deutscher Aktien IndeX)	PAYG	Pay-as-you-go
		PC	Personal Computer
EDV	Electronic Data Processing		
ERP	Enterprise Resource Planning	PIMS	Profit Impact of Marketing Strategy
HR	Human Resources		
		pp.	Pages
HTML	Hypertext Markup Language		
		SaaS	Software as a Service
Iaas	Infrastructure as a Service		
		SAP	Systems, Applications and Products in Data Processing AG
IAO	Institute for work management and organization		
		SLA	Service Level Agreement
IBM	International Business Machines Corporation		
		SMB	Small and Medium sized business
ICT	Information and communications technology		
		SOA	Service-oriented Architecture
IDS	Intrusion detection system	SWOT	Strengths, Weaknesses, Opportunities and Threats
IPS	Intrusion prevention system		
IT	Information Technology	TCO	Total Cost of Ownership
MBA	Master of Business Administration	TÜV	Technischer Überwachungs-Verein
MDM	Mobile Device Management	USA	United States of America
MS	Microsoft Corporation	UTM	Unified Threat Management
MSN	Microsoft Messenger	VoIP	Voice over Internet Protocol

BIBLIOGRAPHY

[1] Baun, Christian; Kunze, Marcel: *Cloud computing: Web-basierte dynamische IT-Services*. Springer, 2010.

[2] Buzzel, Robert D.: *The PIMS program of strategy research. A retrospective appraisal*. Journal of Business Research, 57, 2004, pp. 478-483

[3] European Union: *Commission recommendation concerning the definition of micro, small and medium-sized enterprise*. Official Journal, 2003

[4] Grant, Robert M.: *Contemporary strategy analysis*. Fourth edition, Blackwell publishing, 2002

[5] Hofer, Chuck; Schendel, Dan: *Strategy formulation: Analytical concepts*. St. Paul: West Publishing, 1977

[6] Hoffmann, Mario: *Sicher in der Cloud*. University Journal, 12. volume, April-Mai, 2011

[7] Köhler-Schute, Christiana; et al: *Cloud Computing: Neue Optionen für Unternehmen*. KS Energy Verlag, 2011

[8] Kretschmer, Tobias: *Vernetztes Arbeiten in Wirtschaft und Gesellschaft*. 2010

[9] Holtkamp, Berndhard: *Cloud Computing für den Mittelstand am Beispiel der Logistikbranche*. Fraunhofer ISST, 2010

[10] Metzger, Christian; Reitz, Thorsten; Villar, Juan: *Cloud computing, Chancen und Risiken aus technischer und unternehmerischer Sicht*. Hanser, 2011

[11] Möller, Christian: *Diplomarbeit mit dem Thema Cloud Computing-Einsatz im E-Business*. Grin, 2010

[12] Oetiker, Tobias: *The not so short introduction to LaTeX*. 2011

[13] Porter, Michael E.: *The five competitive forces that shape strategy*. Harvard Business Review, volume January, 2008, p. 4

[14] Rhoton, John: *Cloud Computing Explained*. Recursive Press, 2010

[15] Terplan, Kornel; Voigt, Christian: *Cloud Computing*. mitp, 2011

[16] T-Systems Enterprise Services: *White Paper. Cloud Computing I*. T-Systems, 2011

[17] T-Systems Enterprise Services: *White Paper. Cloud Computing II*. T-Systems, 2011

[18] T-Systems Enterprise Services: *White Paper. Dynamic Services.* T-Systems, 2011

[19] Van Zütphen, Thomas: *Avancen aus der Wolke.* Best Practice - Das Kundenmagazin von T-Systems, volume 01, 2011, pp. 18-21

[20] Van Zütphen, Thomas: *Der CIO als Cloud-Broker.* Das Kundenmagazin von T-Systems, volume 01, 2011, pp. 22-23

[21] Velte, Anthony; Velte, Toby; Elsenpeter, Robert: *Cloud computing: A practical approach.* McGrawHill, 2010

[22] Wamser, Christoph: *Strategisches Electronic Commerce.* Verlag Vahlen, 2001

[23] Weidmann, Monika; Renner, Thomas; Rex, Sascha: *Cloud computing in der Versicherungsbranche.* Fraunhofer IAO, 2010.

Internet sources

[24] Bias, Randy: *Debunking the "No Such Thing as A Private Cloud" Myth,* January 19, 2010. Retrieved February 20, 2012, from `http://www.cloudscaling.com/blog/cloud-computing/debunking-the-no-such-thing-as-a-private-cloud-myth`

[25] Cloud puzzle: *Cloud Puzzle Online Applications and Services Directory,* 2012. Retrieved November 19, 2011, from `http://www.cloudpuzzle.com`

[26] ERP software: *Der Größte unabhängige ERP-Software Vergleich,* 2011. Retrieved November 26, 2011, from `http://www.erp-software.org/erp-software-finden`

[27] Forrester Research: *Cloud computing definition,* 2011. Retrieved February 12, 2012, from `http://www.forrester.com/rb/research`

[28] Gartner Research: *Gartner Says Worldwide Cloud Services Market to Surpass $68 Billion in 2010,* June 22, 2010. Retrieved March 4, 2012, from `http://www.gartner.com/it/page.jsp?id=1389313`

[29] Gartner research: *Gartner says cloud computing will be as influential as E-business,* June 26, 2008. Retrieved February 12, 2012, from `http://www.gartner.com/it/page.jsp?id=707508`

[30] Göldi, Andreas: *Google macht Ernst mit Cloud Computing,* March 11, 2010. Retrieved November 26, 2011, from `ttp://netzwertig.com/2010/03/11/app-marketplace-google-macht-ernst-mit-enterprise-cloud-computing`

[31] Google: *Google Apps for Business,* 2012. Retrieved November 26, 2011, from `http://www.google.com/apps/intl/en/business/index.html`

[32] Google: *Google Apps Marketplace,*2011. Retrieved November 27, 2011, from `http://www.google.com/enterprise/marketplace`

[33] Grohmann, Werner: *Initiative Cloud Services Made in Germany*, 2011. Retrieved November 19, 2011, from `http://www.cloud-services-made-in-germany.de`

[34] IBM corporation: *Unified communications*, 2012. Retrieved March 12, 2012, from `http://www-142.ibm.com/software/products/us/en/category/SWAAA`

[35] Microsoft corporation: *SMB Value, Journey to the Cloud*, 2011. Retrieved February 19, 2012, from `http://www.microsoft.com/business/Office365/webcasts/smb-value-journey-to-the-cloud.asp`

[36] National Institute of Standards and Technology: *NIST Definition of Cloud Computing*, 2011. Retrieved November 19, 2011, from `http://csrc.nist.gov/publications/nistpubs/800-145/SP800-145.pdf`

[37] Open projects software: *Software definition*, 2012. Retrieved March 12, 2012, from `http://www.openprojects.org/software-definition.htm`

[38] PC magazine encyclopedia: *Definition of client/server*, 2012. Retrieved March 4, 2012, from `http://www.pcmag.com/encyclopedia_term/0,2542,t=clientserver&i=39801,00.asp`

[39] PC magazine encyclopedia: *Definition of cloud computing*, 2012. Retrieved March 4, 2012, from `http://www.pcmag.com/encyclopedia`

[40] PC magazine encyclopedia: *Web development software*, 2012. Retrieved March 12, 2012, from `http://www.pcmag.com/encyclopedia_term/0,2542,t=Web+development+software&i=54296,00.asp`

[41] Project management software: *Project management software*, 2011. Retrieved March 12, 2012, from `http://www.projectmanagementsoftware.com`

[42] Salesforce: *The cloud computing marketplace from Salesforce*, 2011. Retrieved November 26, 2011, from `http://appexchange.salesforce.com/home`

[43] Techopedia: *Application suite*, 2012. Retrieved March 12, 2012, from `http://www.techopedia.com/definition/4224/application-software`

[44] Webopedia, IT Business Edge: *Application software definition*, 2012. Retrieved March 12, 2012, from `http://www.webopedia.com/TERM/A/application.html`

[45] Webopedia, IT Business Edge: *Customer relationship management software*, 2012. Retrieved March 12, 2012, from `http://www.webopedia.com/TERM/C/CRM.html`

[46] Webopedia, IT Business Edge: *Enterprise Resource Planning*, 2012. Retrieved March 12, 2012, from `http://www.webopedia.com/TERM/E/ERP.html`

[47] Webopedia, IT Business Edge: *What is mainframe?*, 2012. Retrieved March 4, 2012, from `http://www.webopedia.com/TERM/M/mainframe.html`

[48] Wikipedia: *Client-server model*, 2012. Retrieved March 4, 2012, from `http://en.wikipedia.org/wiki/Client-server_model`

[49] Wikipedia: *Cloud Computing*, 2012. Retrieved February 2, 2012, from `http://en.wikipedia.org/wiki/Cloud_computing`

[50] Wikipedia: *Communication software*, 2012. Retrieved March 8, 2012, from `http://en.wikipedia.org/wiki/Communication_software`

[51] Wikipedia: *Fleet management software*, 2012. Retrieved March 14, 2012, from `http://en.wikipedia.org/wiki/Fleet_management_software`

[52] Wikipedia: *Grossrechner*, 2012. Retrieved March 4, 2012, from `http://de.wikipedia.org/wiki/Grossrechner`

[53] Wikipedia: *Human resource management system*, 2012. Retrieved March 14 2012, from `http://en.wikipedia.org/wiki/Human_resource_management_system`

[54] Wikipedia: *Mittelstand*, 2012. Retrieved March 12 2012, from `http://en.wikipedia.org/wiki/Mittelstand`

[55] Wikipedia: *Procurement software*, 2012. Retrieved March 12, 2012, from `http://en.wikipedia.org/wiki/Procurement_software`

[56] Wikipedia: *Team collaboration software*, 2012. Retrieved March 12, 2012, from `http://en.wikipedia.org/wiki/Collaborative_software`